Journey to Compostela

Journey to Compostela

A Novel of Medieval Pilgrimage and Peril

Bernard Reilly

COMBINED PUBLISHING
Pennsylvania

PUBLISHER'S NOTE

The headquarters of Combined Publishing are located midway between Valley Forge and the Germantown battlefield, on the outskirts of Philadelphia. From its beginnings, our company has been steeped in the oldest traditions of American history and publishing. Our historic surroundings help maintain our focus on history and our books strive to uphold the standards of style, quality and durability first established by the earliest bookmakers of Germantown and Philadelphia so many years ago. Our famous monk-and-console logo reflects our commitment to the modern and yet historic enterprise of publishing.

We call ourselves Combined Publishing because we have always felt that our goals could only be achieved through a "combined" effort by authors, publishers and readers. We have always tried to maintain maximum communication between these three key players in the reading experience.

We are always interested in hearing from prospective authors about new books in our field. We also like to hear from our readers and invite you to contact us at our offices in Pennsylvania with any questions, comments or suggestions, or if you have difficulty finding our books at a local bookseller.

For information, address:
Combined Publishing
P.O. Box 307
Conshohocken, PA 19428
E-mail: combined@combinedpublishing.com
Web: www.combinedpublishing.com
Orders: 1-800-418-6065

Cataloging-in-Publication Data available from the Library of Congress.

ISBN 1-58097-042-7

Printed in the United States of America.

Dedication

To our grandchildren.
May the past resonate for them.

Chronology

Compostela
Lugo
Oviedo
Leon
Astorga
Sahagún
Burgos
Pamplona
Jaca
Zamora
Segovia
Barcelona
Tarragona
Salamanca
Avila
Toledo
Lisbon
Cordoba
Seville

Medieval Spain

Journey to Compostela

Chapter One

The damp of his clothing was still pervasive but the real chill had drained away. He wasn't sure exactly when. Like the bite of the frost in ones fingers and toes, one moment it was there and the next it was gone, without stirring a consciousness of its departure.

Beginning to feel the slight heat of the morning sun on his back, he sat up and rearranged his cloak across his shoulders but kept his chin buried on his chest. His eyes were closed, although the wide brim of the great hat would have provided shadow anyway. Sitting upright had eased the ache of his back and hips but he had no desire to come full awake. Dozing at this hour was the last precious indulgence he would have before the slide into sleep that would follow a supper that seemed far off now.

"Lift your head, pilgrim! Greet the world! Salute your betters!"

No more than half-conscious still, Martin tilted back his head, blinking against the light, to see four hooves planted in the dust. He must have slept again. As he watched, a chased-steel spearhead dropped down into his line of vision until it

13

hung in the air only a hand's breadth away from his face. Now he was fully awake. His hair prickled on the back of his neck and his guts doubled within him.

Very, very gradually, Martin raised his head, being careful to move no other portion of his body. Astride the dun-colored palfrey before him was a young man of twenty-two or twenty-three years. He wore a riding tunic of pale green picked with red cockatoos. His boots were of finely crafted doeskin that showed no wear even where they entered the stirrups. The young man's blond hair was caught in a ribboned plait that hung to the middle of his back. The extended left arm that held the six-foot oak shaft behind the spearhead was only slightly tanned and the hand that gripped the spear wore no fewer than three gold rings. That spearhead still hung absolutely quiet. Without effort the young man kept it just before Martin's eyes. He could detect not the slightest movement.

The eyes that met Martin's were so pale a blue that they almost merged with the whites. Beneath them his long, straight nose just failed to overhang thin lips, now bent into the faintest of smiles. There was no real mirth in it—only amusement perhaps.

"You are bold, farmer. You have not yet risen as I told you and you make bold to look me full in the face. I would take that badly if you were not so sleep-fuddled. Roust yourself, tender of cattle."

The man's voice was not loud but it conveyed a threat. Martin very slowly thrust himself up from the ground, getting his legs under him carefully. As he did so, the spearhead followed. It never wavered more than a hand away from his face.

"So you do have legs, bumpkin. Tell us your business. Why do you sit becloaked next to the trail, like a great lump of ordure? You could offend our ladies."

"I slept here, sire. I am a pilgrim to Compostela, or would

14

be, and I was waiting here to join some band coming down from the town."

"Ah? I took you to be from beyond the mountains. You do speak a kind of French. But I think that you did not come over the pass back there by yourself. Have you murdered your companions then? Do you sit here waiting for some other hapless idiots to rob and kill in their sleep?"

"No, my lord, I am a man of peace. I had a farm in the valley of Comminges beyond the mountains. I sold it and joined some merchants coming over the Somport Pass who were on their way to trade for ivory in Zaragoza. But they stopped just behind you in Jaca to drink and gamble. By the time they finished, they had lost all their trade goods so they went home again to rebuild their stocks. I came down here to wait for another band heading west. Two or three of the tavern owners of the town can vouch for my story."

"Do I look like a magistrate? Am I to interrogate some stinking publican about a bum I found by the side of the road? I know you are a man of peace, farmer. That's because you don't have the talent for war—or the belly for it either, probably. Well, you've found your pilgrimage. Gather up those rags and join the band. I recruited them. They'll be happy that I've recruited you to share their troubles."

This was no request, no invitation. Martin knew there would be none. Nor did the spearhead cease to hang, motionless, just before his face. Reading the cold glint in the knight's eyes, he chose. Martin wordlessly started to stuff his knapsack with his groundsheet and blanket as the other man neck-reined his palfrey away and turned towards the west at an easy gait.

Martin stood aside as the caravan trooped after the blond youth. A heavy, short groom and a slighter, younger servant led two magnificent stallions, keeping them well apart and straining against their tackle. The horses were grey as fine steel with snowy manes and black stockings on all four legs. If they had not had the same stallion for father they had a common mare as mother. The stallions danced through the turn west, making a small dust cloud.

At a careful distance they were trailed by another youth, perhaps fifteen, and missing a left eye. As he passed Martin, he swiveled his head awkwardly to focus his remaining eye on the newcomer. But he spoke no word and quickly resumed the management of two dusky asses whose leads he jerked with some regularity. Both animals were fairly loaded. The travel cover concealed the burden of the one but the other bore a long lance, point behind, two sheathed swords, two hunting bows, and no fewer than five quivers of arrows. All this gear was strapped about another travel cover which Martin guessed protected an assortment of body armor.

They were followed a respectful distance behind the lance point by three two-wheeled carts drawn by teams of longhorned oxen. In the first of these rode a round, brown little man whose coweled black robe with small suspended cross marked him as a cleric of some type. Martin slung his pack into the cart as it lumbered abreast and then heaved himself over the side. The driver made no objection and offered no greeting. Contrasting oddly with the character of the driver, the tripods and cauldrons which comprised most of the obvious contents of the cart announced it as a cook's vehicle. Sitting on one of the overturned pots, Martin surveyed the company which he had just been persuaded to join.

Two remaining carts jolting along were driven by the ordinary sort of drover. Their contents were in part obscured by covers but also held a scattering of knapsacks. Doubtless these belonged to some of the pilgrims strung out behind them. These latter were difficult to characterize. They appeared to number fifty or sixty persons, most wearing large travel cloaks and broad-brimmed hats that concealed much of their features. None of them were mounted or led beasts except for three men at the very tail of the procession who walked beside asses loaded with burdens.

After this cursory survey, Martin turned toward the driver. The latter was a good head shorter than his new passenger but was almost twice as broad. His capped head was very round and closeshaven. His robe appeared to be of good wool and, to look at, had not been mended often.

"I'm Martin," the passenger offered. "I had a farm not long ago but I sold it after my wife died and made up my mind to do the pilgrimage to Santiago de Compostela."

"You might have fallen in with better company," was the short reply of the little priest. He didn't bother to turn his head.

"I didn't have a choice," said Martin. "You must have seen how I came to join you."

"No more choice than the rest of us. My name is Simon."

Since the priest had at least volunteered his name, Martin was encouraged to continue.

"I make it from your clothes that you are a priest—if they are your own clothes. How does it happen that a priest passes his time driving an oxcart?"

"Call it a penance, if you will. Back there at the end of this procession are my man, my ass, and my possessions. You can make them out."

For the first time the driver turned his head and his passenger could see an almost perfectly round, sunburned little face, set with an equally tiny nose, eyes like black stones, and a wide, thin-lipped mouth. It was, Martin thought, not an unpleasant, but a serious, visage, that had a certain melancholy gravity about it.

Despite himself, Martin grinned. "That's a kind of penance I never saw before now. Who set you to it, your bishop? Are you supposed to drive this cart all the way to the western sea?"

Simon looked at Martin long and steadily. The oxen were plodding along over level, rutted dirt and required only the slightest attention from their driver. Finally the priest's eyebrows went up as his chin sunk toward his chest. There was not much neck to separate them.

"My bishop in Limoges authorized the pilgrimage, to be sure, but gave no directions about my becoming a drayman. That humiliation was devised by our present leader. You have already met him. He is a knight from Angers. His name is Rainald but he might better be called 'old Nick.'"

All of this was said in a voice not much above a whisper. Martin had the feeling that he was being taken into a confidence, that he was being invited to become an ally rather than a friend. He no more wanted to become a party to a dispute already in progress than he had wished an hour ago to join this band. Still, he needed to know something more about the company into which he had been thrown so abruptly and the priest seemed to be the perfect person to explain such things to him—if he would.

"Your knight would seem an unlikely sort to lead a pilgrimage. Arrogance such as his sits uneasily with penance, I should think. And why would he choose to humiliate you? That was the word you chose."

"Because it was my pilgrimage!" The words came in a rush but still in a furtive tone. "I organized it in Limoges. I and a young priest, Gerald, did so. Together we got the bishop's blessing and preached it to the townspeople and those of the surrounding countryside. Just before we were ready to depart, that devil rode in with his retainers. He asked to join us very politely. He offered to protect us along the road and, as no one else in the group had much experience with fighting, it seemed like a good idea to let him come along. Now that he has taken control of it entirely, it amuses him to harass me, its former leader. My misfortunes are a daily warning to the rest of the band."

"And what about your friend Gerald? Has some equal trial been devised for him?"

The little priest looked away. When he spoke, his voice was even, flat, and controlled.

"Gerald is gone. I'm sure he is dead, God protect him. Rainald killed him."

Martin found his throat suddenly dry. He knew nothing about it but he was sure that Simon was right. He could almost visualize the murder. It would have been passionless, cold. For just that reason he had to protest against the voicing of such a thing.

"Do you know what you say to be true? You didn't see it. Perhaps your friend just crept off one night. He saw the course that things were taking, saw that he couldn't change them, and just left."

The priest had not complained. He did not now. He gazed at the newcomer with sadness that bespoke sympathy.

"Gerald was a strong young man. He resisted the little advances, the suggestions that began to be made after we had been on the road for a score of days. He protested the gradual usurpations in small things: the time for morning departures; the time for making camp of an evening; the choice of sites. The knight simply smiled his cold smile and ignored him. It was easy enough for he and his servants to intimidate the rest of the party. Each day Gerald and I had less and less influence with the group and the knight had more. One morning when we woke on the banks of the Oloron, my friend was gone. There was no blanket, no knapsack, nothing. They killed him in the night and threw his body and his goods into the river."

The cart jolted violently and almost stopped. Left to themselves, the oxen had walked its left wheel into a half-buried stone that gave momentary pause even to their stolid strength. Martin jumped down and walked beside the wheel for a dozen paces. It seemed uninjured but it would bear looking after. If its shaped timbers had separated even a little, the crack would get worse unless it could be patched.

Martin could see the knight riding back down the line past the extra horses. The palfrey was pulled up and wheeled just a little too close. The pedestrian had to look to his feet.

"Trouble, farmer? Your driver is careless. But perhaps he is not accustomed to such sudden friendships. Perhaps you presume on his solitude. These men of God like their long silences and their lonely vigils. It would be kinder to him if you were to walk. Safer too. Let him give his whole attention to the oxen."

The knight smiled without warmth and wheeled his horse, again too closely, and rode off to regain his position at the head of the band. Martin walked for the rest of the day's march. He thought of dropping back to take the temper of the rest of the group but decided against it, because he knew that he was being warned off the priest. Claire had always said that he was stubborn and that he made them trouble by it. She had been right. Yet stubbornness was sometimes all a man had left.

Chapter Two

Four days of walking settled Martin into the necessary routine. The rhythm was the essential thing: to set one foot before the other without thought, without conciousness of the act, and to continue in that fashion for hours. That way the ground flowed into the distance behind and you didn't fight to cover it. Your mind was left free to ponder anything—or nothing—and restrained from useless calculations of the physical difficulties ahead or even already present. Funny that one's body so many times and in so many ways should function better when one's mind had forgotten it.

Not that this was a bad stretch. The purple and white and gold of the Pyrenees to the north stretched along the right side of the column with a majestic presence that soothed the head and spirit. At least that was so now that one no longer had to anticipate scaling them. Martin was grateful for the cooling breeze that blew intermittently down from their gorges and high valleys. It provided an alternation of solace and stimulus to the steady heat, even so soon being supplied by the spring sunshine. Still, it made for damn cold nights too.

Most of the column of pilgrims exhibited the same detachment from the actual business of walking. At least those who had some likelihood of actually reaching Santiago de Compostela did. Martin had an opportunity to ferret out a little information about the earlier part of the journey, before he had joined them outside of Jaca. Their experience had been much the same as that he had observed traveling down to that town with the merchants. People didn't last. Whatever impulse first moved them to join the pilgrimage and to leave their homes, often faded before they ever struck the rhythm that might have maintained them. The initial, grinding efforts made them reconsider that decision and suggested other, unexpected difficulties that might await them. Sooner or later, they simply slipped away at night and went back home.

Then too, there were the careless ones—those who didn't look to their feet until it was too late. A bad shoe could be a hell on earth for sustained walking. Of course, anyone could turn an ankle, even break it. Either one meant that you were left by the side of the road. If you mended you could join the next group to come along. But most often the misfortune was just the last of a number of mishaps and your resolve was gone. You stayed where you had dropped out and found a new life there if you were lucky. Or someone knocked you on the head, for such of your gear as remained, and your troubles were over for good. Or you eventually straggled back home to be jeered as a fool.

The story of this group was just like most, Martin learned. A good dozen and a half of those who had started had already left or had been left. And still there were those that Martin doubted would make the full journey out to the shrine of the Apostle. And who knew how many would ever make the trek back? He had no real confidence that he himself would ever come back along this trail—or any other.

The squat, burly groom, Robert, probably would not get so far as the western ocean. Managing two blooded stallions on such a march had a great likelihood of leaving him crippled or dead somewhere along the route. Already the heavier of the two horses had managed to catch the groom's foot, although only to bruise it. Both of the brutes lashed out at him from time to time with their hooves, hoping to take him off guard. Sooner or later they would succeed unless he neglected the close care of them—and there was little chance that his knightly master would allow him such liberty. When the stallions should manage to injure or cripple Robert, he could expect little sympathy from the rest of the group whom he bullied and who responded with cordial, if concealed, hatred.

Ermentrude too was as good as dead if Martin was any judge of such things. The woman was overly tall. She topped Robert by a full head. Worse yet, her feet were flat. While it would be too much to call her fat, her solidly muscled body weighed too heavily on those poor extremities. Already she panted and winced with the incessant plodding, though she did not complain. One day she would simply cease to be able to walk and then would be left somewhere along the path. If she were lucky the natives would kill her quickly, but it was more likely she would be raped soundly before they finished her. The tall Fleming would not even be able to protest in a language her molestors would understand. Most of the other pilgrims had trouble following her heavy North French dialect.

A few days ago he had asked her directly, "Ermentrude, what are you doing on such a pilgrimage without a husband or brother to protect you?"

She had regarded him stolidly, peering out from under heavy brows and over those high cheekbones.

"I have no husband. Never had. My brothers are long dead."

"But you must have known that you would run a good chance of losing your life on a journey like this."

"I lost my life when my older sister married. Her new husband made our farm his own and decided that I was more beast than kin. If he had not possessed a good ox team he would probably have hitched me to his plow. Suddenly my sister, my companion, was made my mistress. All work was too heavy for her but lightness itself for me. So it went. I could have become her rival. He would have plowed me, just as he did our land and my sister, readily enough—but I forswore that. Plain as I am I have my pride. So I left."

"You would have done better to seek a husband."

"Without a dowry? Without even a milk cow or a pair of sheep? Man, I'm already thirty-six seasons. Even to drop someone's child at my age would likely kill me. Should I have sought a love match? Look at me!"

It was true. With her straw-colored hair wrapped tight about her head, with her flat features and large mouth, she was no beauty. Her large hands and feet and heavy body might make her a substantial help on a farm, but farmers like himself wanted something of an inheritance anyway. If you had land yourself, those who would mate with you needed to bring something to the union beside simple greed. Such thoughts made him uncomfortable and so he avoided her thereafter.

Martin himself was feeling younger. Twenty years of farming had left their mark. His land never had been really good. Wet, heavy soil made heavy, grueling work. He had never produced such a good crop as would have let him buy a first-rate plow team, or even a part share in one. He had plowed with bad, spavined animals and had made up for their failings with the hoe. That was how one made do, if one was poor. Not so poor, God forbid, as the landless lot. Just always on the edge of want.

Now he was free of it. Mere walking was so light an effort that he would lose his strength if he were not careful. But then, what did he need it for anyway? For the first time he could remember since childhood, he had no worries beyond a warm place to sleep the coming night. He had no seed to get in the ground, no weeds to fight, no crop to rot in the rain—if it should rain. Despite himself, he felt like a boy. A boy, at thirty-three years! Maybe it was the last time ever but he could not but smile to himself in the sheer enjoyment of it.

For some time the building on the right flank of the little column had been resolving itself more and more clearly. By now one could surmise that it was a monastery-church, a fine stone monastery of fairly new workmanship and impressive size. It sat like an eagle's nest on a broad ledge high above the road west and the river that the road followed. Ahead, the knight Rainald turned into the rutted path leading up toward the structure and signaled with an arm that the pilgrims were to do likewise. Almost immediately a kind of excitement stirred in the column. The day's march had not yet reached the noon hour and there was prospect of a break in the routine.

"The lord wants you, farmer."

From the beginning the groom had adopted the arrogance and language of his master towards Martin.

"Me? What for?"

For some little time now the pilgrim band had been resting, talking, eating a little as they spread about the level ground behind the monastic buildings and just before the fringes of the tall escarpment that rose to the north. The knight himself had gone off after they were settled, towards a thatched, wooden structure that could be guessed to be the quarters of the lord abbot of the place. On Rainald's approach, there had been a flurry in the small knot of men that stood about the door and then a tiny man had emerged who was rapidly seated on a stool placed in the shade at the side of the building. Another stool had been offered the knight and now the two sat facing one another.

"How would I know? He said to come and get you and so I have. Just shut your mouth and come along."

The groom turned away in the direction of his master and the abbot while Martin followed him. It would be foolish to take offense at the brusqueness of the man-at-arms, and anyway, he was curious.

The tall knight half turned as Martin came up. As always Rainald's manner was languid, his voice low and almost expressionless. There was, Martin thought, a hint of impatience that escaped the other's usual control.

"We seem to need your help, friend. The lord abbot here knows no French and I can make no sense of the country patois they speak hereabouts. You lived just over the mountains. See if you can make him understand me."

Martin turned toward the abbot, a tiny old man, browned and wizened, who fairly blended with the shadow of his black cowl and robe. The cleric could not have reached to his shoulder, even standing.

"Greetings, father. This good French chevalier and knight, Rainald by name, asks me to convey to you his greetings and good wishes."

He spoke in the language of the mountains familiar to him from the shepherds and hunters of his home district. The diminutive abbot replied in the same tongue.

"And you may return to your master my welcome and good wishes. My own given name is Sancho and I am abbot here of the monastery-church of San Salvador of Leire. In what can we be of service?"

Martin glanced toward the knight.

"We can make ourselves understood to one another, sire. He is the abbot here and makes you welcome. His name is Sancho."

"Don't be puffed-up, bumpkin. It is a small enough talent

for countryfolk to understand countryfolk. Ask the lord abbot if it is permitted to spend the day here refreshing ourselves from our journey."

Martin turned again toward the little cleric.

"As your worship doubtless sees we are pilgrims on the road to Compostela. The knight who leads us requests permission to rest here for the remainder of the day."

"Indeed, he already seems to have presumed it," came the response. "And his men-at-arms have surveyed our little grounds and modest buildings. But you are welcome, to be sure. Are you positive that your master understands no word of what we speak?"

Martin was startled by the question and its implication. He smiled and pretended to be puzzled for a moment.

"He is a warrior and a man of quick wits as well as a quick sword, sir. I think that he does not understand us but he does watch us closely."

Then, turning to Rainald, he continued.

"The lord abbot is glad to proffer the use of his lands, sire. He would ask if he may be of further service."

"Does he now? Tell him that I would be pleased to have him inspect my stallions. They are full-blooded animals that could do much to improve the quality of the monastery stock or that of his house's clients in the country round about. I should be happy to put them to stud for their benefit. I would, of course, expect that such a service would be repaid in some fashion, since we have gone to the considerable trouble to bring them over the mountains."

The abbot sat impassively as this message was relayed. Then he smiled and spread his hands in self-deprecation.

"I am curious to know what sort of man employs a priest of God as a driver of one of his animal carts. Do you think that your master could be moved to reconsider such a shameful practice? But for now, tell him that we are a poor house here. I would be interested to see his stallions but we possess only a few asses and some oxen that could hardly benefit from their services. Moreover, as he can see for himself by looking about the countryside, this is not a rich district and our humble tenants here are in much the same straits."

"The knight is not my master—though I am forced to accompany him for now. If I know him, he would likely receive your rebuke most violently. Be careful."

Then, turning again to Rainald, Martin told him of the abbot's reaction to his offer of stud.

The knight replied with some impatience.

"Poor is he? He's damn well not poor in words. And the two of you chatter like jays. Keep what you say brief, farmer. Ask him, if the community is so poor, how does it come to have a splendid, almost new church?"

"Take care with what you say or do, my lord abbot." Martin frowned as he put the query and followed it with his own advice. Though he continued to show no emotion, the monk's response told the interpreter that he had grasped the essentials of the situation.

"Tell the lord knight that we are blessed with royal protection here. King Sancho has been pleased to support the building of a new monastery church because his grandfather, his namesake, awaits the resurrection of the dead in our house. The great King Sancho of Navarra, dead some forty-odd years, was the greatest king in anyone's memory. He ruled not only this smallish land but the land of castles to the south of it and even the better part of the kingdom of Leon itself. His dominion reached out almost to the mountains of Galicia and to the banks of the Duero River. Most of that was lost on his death but he now has a worthy grandson and those days may yet come again.

"Meanwhile, we are privileged to offer prayers daily for the king and his ancestors to the benefit of their souls. I would be pleased to show the lord knight the tomb of that great king and to have him share in our worship on the morrow. Doubtless our present king has heard of your passage through our land and will be pleased to learn that you have so honored the mortal remains of his grandfather."

Rainald shifted restlessly as he recieved the abbot's statement. His eyes fixed hard on Martin's.

"Do you play me false, bumpkin? I would kill you for such daring. But if what the old man says is true, then he probably will get to keep his trinkets, don't you think? In any event, I'll take a look at his honored corpse and its treasures and decide then. Tell him that we'll be happy to participate in paying honor to the memory of a great king before we depart in the morning."

Again the new response of the abbot indicated that he had understood the unspoken danger.

"It occurs to us that the good knight may want to offer his services directly to our king. Our master's rule goes extremely well just now. Not long ago he participated with the great king of the Leonese, Alfonso, in the avenging of the treacherous murder of his cousin, king of Navarra. As a result, our King Sancho's lands now stretch almost to the Ebro River in the west. You will be traveling through them until you reach those of the Leonese Alfonso. Either now, or when the good knight returns from his pilgrimage, he might want to spend some time in our king's service. Our sovereign is a lord generous to the valiant and he plans to drive the Muslims to the south back farther from our lands."

Rainald drily thanked the cleric for his news. The interview ended then, after a further brief exchange of formalities. On the morning that followed, the abbot allowed the attendance of the entire pilgrim band at the conventual Mass and some of the latter made small offerings from what little they had to the upkeep of the shrine. Rainald viewed this with barely disguised contempt.

Later, during their departure, the abbot seemed to pay particular attention to the priest, Simon. The eyes of the warrior sought Martin's in question.

"You and I will talk, farmer. You are not as stupid as I first thought. On the whole, that makes it even more unlikely that you will get as far as Compostela before I have to kill you. Remember that."

Chapter Three

Stars covered the vault of the heavens in lavish display. The wind off the mountains had risen shortly after the setting of the sun. Those pilgrims who usually would have retreated to their bedrolls still hung about the fringes of the campfire savoring its warmth, illuminated by the light of a full moon as well as the blaze's restless tongues.

The girl stood uneasily at the farthest reach of that circle. Clearly she was greedy for a share in its comfort but was less than sure what welcome the group might afford her. Restlessly she shifted from foot to foot, reluctant to withdraw or to approach more closely.

She was a slight thing of not more than a dozen years. Her eyes and hair were dark and liquid. Her brown skin matched the somber hue of the poor cloak that partially covered a short tunic of the same color and condition. Martin noticed that she wore a ring that appeared to be of worked gold with a green stone of some sort.

While considerably younger than most, the girl was obviously one of those women who regularly came into the pilgrim camps after nightfall to prospect for what might be had in return for their favors. They were sent by their fathers or their mothers, sometimes even by their husbands. Life in the foothills of the Pyrenees was spare and grinding for farming families. Every asset had to be put to use. Pilgrim bands, such as theirs, offered a rare chance to steal, to sell, to barter. The road to Santiago became, in season, a market four hundred miles long, stretching from the mountains behind them to the western sea. It supported every sort of business imaginable.

Like most such groups, these pilgrims were largely male. By this point in the long journey the first fervor of religion had slackened somewhat. Then too, not everyone in the band had had a religious motive to begin with. In any event, they almost all still boasted some little store of goods or wealth to sustain them through the trip, but could be parted from some portion of it if the right incentive was proffered. That such women as this should materialize out of the night had become a common experience by now. The priest, Simon, had taken notice of her and was just withdrawing quietly into the dark. There was no way for him to control this sort of traffic and so it was better simply not to be present.

By now, the figure of the girl had caught the attention of the groom, Robert, as well. Grinning, he beckoned to her.

"Come in, girl. We'll share our fire with you. This is a poor lot but you're welcome to a little of everything I have."

She looked about the group but no one else spoke. What that burly figure had said she had no idea but his gesture was clear enough. Smiling, as if to apologize for it, she walked a few paces closer to the fire. She was shivering slightly. From the wind and from fear as well. She stood at first, as a doe might, poised for flight. Then she yielded slightly to the solace of the fire and some of the tension went out of her thin body. The girl began to turn the ring on her finger, as if it were a new possession and this her first opportunity to examine it carefully.

"That's a pretty prize, darling. Give us a look at what you've won."

The knight's ostler extended his hand towards the native girl and the dark child shrank back from his tone and manner. Robert's voice came more harshly now.

"Don't be coy, you little bitch. We all know where you got that trinket and how you got it. You didn't think that you'd finished earning it already, did you? You just come right over here to a real man and give him a look. Then I'll tell you what it will cost you to finish paying for it."

The groom came to his feet. He leered at the others seated about the fire but found no response from them. Most chose to stare uneasily into the flames.

The young woman was genuinely alarmed now. She too glanced at the figures seated about the fire and that was her mistake. With a swiftness that belied his bulk, Robert stepped forward and seized her by the hand that wore the ring. He jerked her toward him, raising the hand to peer at the jewel.

"By God, that's a fine present for such a skinny little bitch. Not much to you but you must have served him well to have been rewarded so handsomely. Still, I'm afraid you'll have to spend the whole night with me to work off the rest of its price."

The young woman tried to pull her hand free. Terrified, her voice came in small, unintelligible and juvenile pleading—half moan, half sob. Her feet scrabbled in the dirt but the resistance of her thin body had no effect against the solid bulk of her captor. Robert's face twisted into a mix of menace and lust.

"So we're a picky little whore, are we? Well, life can't be all blond-headed gentlemen in soft furs and smelling of sweet scents. You can share some of what's left over with a plain man who smells of honest horse sweat."

The big groom twisted her arm behind her and pulled her toward him. With his other hand he grasped her hair and began to jerk her head roughly back and forth to end her resistance. The girl's face was wet and her body shook unevenly with a low, animal intensity.

The sharpness of the crack took them all by surprise.

While they had been frozen by the drama before them, Ermentrude had risen and picked up a short, stout bough from the reserve destined for the night's fire. Then she stepped around the flames and behind the ostler. She was taller than he. Intent on the girl, he never sensed her presence. The Flemish woman swung the branch in a descending arc into the back of the man's neck.

Robert's hands dropped away from the native girl. Ermentrude swung the piece of wood again into the nape of the man's neck and his knees began to buckle. She swung yet again and missed completely as the bulky figure pitched forward onto the ground. She stepped over his form, panting with the exertion, and continued to strike at Robert's head and neck. Martin finally stayed her arm and took the weapon from her hand.

He pushed her away from the unconscious groom. Then he rolled the latter over and placed his hand against his chest. Feeling nothing, Martin bent his head close to the man's mouth and nose. He could detect no trace of breathing. Robert's eyes were open but vacant. Now he began to stink.

Rising, Martin looked at the big pilgrim woman.

"You pole-axed him for sure. He's dead."

She looked at him, dully, making no sound. The native girl had vanished into the dark. Some of the men around the fire had crept off already. They had seen enough and reckoned that no good could come of it.

But at the far edge of the fire's light, the knight Rainald stood and surveyed the scene.

*   *   *

Very early, before full dawn, Simon, the priest, began a hurried Mass for the soul of the dead ostler. He knew full well that the knight would regard it as foolishness and so he wanted to complete the ritual before the latter should come to see what was delaying the day's departure. Then too, the one-eyed groom, Bertran, had discovered the Breton dead in his ragged bedcloths.

The skinny deceased had walked farther than any of them. He had come into their midst by chance when they were first organizing the pilgrimage. He had not asked to join but had simply walked along with them. No one understood anything but the few, spare words of French that the little man could use. He himself had seemed content that it be so. For the last two weeks, however, the quiet Celt had been growing more and more gaunt. He had gradually shrunk inside his rags until it seemed there was hardly enough flesh left on the man to connect one bone to the other. He lurched occasionally but never fell. He slept apart and heavily from last light to dawn.

Now he was dead, as silently as he had lived. No one knew his history, but a search of his meager clothing revealed that he had had some reserves of money. Some eighty pennies were divided more or less evenly among the band as had become the custom when anyone without kin or companion died. His body then had hastily been carried up and laid alongside that of Robert.

After the brief service there was a scramble to find tools to bury the two. Most of what laid about in the bed of the carts was woodcutting stuff and hammers and chisels to repair the wagon wheels that continually threatened to fall off or crack and often delayed the day's march for hours. There was some smithing equipment that was iron-pointed and this was now pressed into use. The soil was poor and thin and was easily moved. But this close to the mountains it was full of stones and small boulders and the light was not sufficiently advanced to make working them loose a simple matter. They had decided, after some argument, that separate graves would be proper for the burial of Christians, though indeed no one was entirely sure that the Breton had been one.

"That can wait for now. You will want a third hole in any event and in a bit the light will be better."

The knight had come upon them unobserved. Instinctively they drew back a step or two. Now, as he turned silently, they followed him to the bed of ashes where the night's fire had been. Ermentrude had sat there through the brief Mass without motion or word, forearms upon her knobby knees, palms clasped before her, head bowed. They were not quite sure whether she had slept or had suffered there the whole night. The group formed a half-circle behind her.

Rainald regarded the woman silently until, unwilling, she was forced to raise her gaze by the very force of his person.

"There is no law or judge here in this strange land that has jurisdiction over a wandering Flemish hag, woman. You fall to me then, since I am leader here and responsible for the good order of this entire company. More than that, I am the aggrieved—since it was my groom that you slew."

"I did not mean to kill him. But it is hard to grieve his death. He deserved to die."

The knight's words came in a monotone. The tall warrior's lips slid into a small, crooked smile.

"You are judge of that? You presume much."

"You were not there, lord. He would have stolen the ring, the gift that you yourself had made to her. He would have taken from her by force the same favors that she had already

36

bestowed on you. She was terrified and struggling—so that he might even have killed her."

"But you made yourself guardian of my property and her body. You fool! Do you think that my own groom would have dared to act so without having first asked my permission? You are a stupid woman who meddles in matters reserved for her betters. However I choose to amuse myself, it is not for you to judge."

Ermentrude blanched. Only slowly did her face come to reveal the appreciation of the full cruelty of the previous night's episode. The knight had set a trap. The girl had been the bait, not the victim. Whom had he planned to ensnare? Not herself, she thought. The priest? The groom himself? Anyone with daring enough to interfere? Did he care? Slowly her face began to register something like anger. She did not speak but her demeanor stiffened and hardened.

Rainald caught the subtle change and his smile spread just perceptibly.

"So now truly you presume to judge me, woman." There was real anger in his voice for the first time.

"So high do you seek to rise for a spinster beloved of no man, possessed of no property, endowed with no grace of mind or body. In your solitary wisdom you would find me guilty of—what? Am I a cruel man; heartless? Perhaps I am possessed of a devil? Perhaps I am unworthy even of your prayers? Do you pray, madam?

"Then pray to your God that you find my mercy. I am disposed to be merciful but justice must be served in some small measure. I will make you a bargain, old woman. I will spare you a hanging, and these diggers in the earth the making of another grave if you will agree to care for my two stallions until we reach the western sea. After all, that is what Robert would have done. Agreed?"

That momentary glitter of hatred, if it had dared to be hatred, faded now from Ermentrude's eyes. Her head dropped and she began by degrees to shudder. The shaking wracked her whole bony, spare frame. The knight regarded her with something like amused contempt.

"So our fine lady is quicker to judgment than to honest toil? Do you admit your incapacity to remedy the loss, the wrong that you have inflicted upon me? What is to be done then?"

Raising his arms as well as his voice, the knight addressed the group. He surveyed them slowly and each of them carefully avoided his eyes.

"What the lady requires is a champion. She needs a good, strong man to fill her lack. She wants someone to pay her debt to me by the care of my stallions. If such a one exists in this fine company I will accept his service in lieu of her own and the lady may live so long as that service is duly performed. Otherwise we must find a stout rope and a high branch for this woman is tall."

His tone mocked and his eyes sparked. He enlarged his contempt to include the entire company before him. He meant to humiliate them in the death of this woman.

"I will care for your horses in the woman's stead."

Just that quickly those near Martin drew back a little from him. For an instant, Rainald himself was startled. Then his composure flowed back and the ironic smile reasserted itself.

"They are stallions, farmer, not 'horses.' They would rend your flesh and kick apart your bones. These are beasts of good blood and brave spirit. You would be no match for them."

"I only offer what you have asked to spare the woman's life. But I have bred my cows to bulls and have survived to talk of it. And I still walk without a limp and all my bones are sound and straight. Bulls are more vicious than your horses I think."

"But more stupid, farmer, more stupid. Like yourself. You will not last two weeks."

"Perhaps so, my lord. But I ask only that you try me. The offer was yours and I have accepted it in good faith."

"In good faith! By all means, let us have good faith here. We are all Christians on pilgrimage together to realize the purging of our sins, are we not? We must be certain that you yourself are moved solely by compassion. We hope that you do not make such an outwardly generous offer with inward carnal designs on this tender virgin. You would not purchase her life to the loss of her immortal soul."

Rainald was mocking them both without surrendering his power over Ermentrude. Though the pretense was transparent, he did not fear that anyone would challenge it. Nor did anyone dare to smirk at his play at solemnity. His eyes were bright and no one wished to become the new target of his whim.

"My lord, I wish only to pay the woman's debt to you. Nothing more."

"The payment of a woman's debt is the act of a husband, farmer. Do you have holy wedlock in mind? I myself would advise you against it. Look at her. Do you doubt that she will be dead long before we reach the western sea? As you can see her beauty has already faded. Her bones are dry. Most probably her flesh will be cold and withered to the touch as well. You strike a poor bargain, farmer. A woman should bring something splendid to the marriage bed and I do not see that this Flemish virago possesses either property or charm to reward your generosity. Perhaps you would like to think yet again?"

Martin surprised himself in that he chose not to answer. He understood the risk in even so mild a resistance. Yet there was a humiliation to which he would not submit. More, there was a humiliation to which he would not let the woman be subjected. The silence between Martin and the knight grew and the assembled pilgrims stirred uneasily as they felt that tension. This was an ugly thing, promising blood if not soon ended.

Ermentrude intervened. "I accept the kind offer of brother Martin, lord, just as he has made it. So long only that, if I die during this journey as you have predicted, he will be quit of all obligation to you."

Rainald was tired of this play. It had stretched out beyond his envisioning and had taken a form that could make him appear ridiculous, though no one would venture to maintain such a view openly. It was time to end the farce for the present. His prey was not likely to escape, in any event.

"My dear woman, farmer Martin will never be quit of obligation to me now. And do not presume to fancy that your miserable carcass has the slightest to do with it. Be grateful that you will not likely live to see how this little bargain between your champion and I is ended."

Abruptly his words lashed out at the group of witnesses.

"It is well past first light. Put those two into the ground quickly now. Bertran, show brother Martin where my beauties are hobbled and help to keep him alive till day's end at least. I shall want to leave soon, very soon."

And so it was. The group could not move quickly enough in its haste to escape what had promised to be another death. Never since their departure from Angers had the camp been struck so quickly and with such hearty good will.

Chapter Four

The stallions hated one another. Merely that another one like himself should exist was intolerable to each. For the favors of Dido, Rainald's palfrey and the only mare with the pilgrimage, they were both exclusive suitors. But the knight required Martin to keep the big males away from his ordinary mount. He believed that their enforced celibacy would make them more spirited, evil in disposition, and terrible in battle if it came to that—and quicker to stud when that opportunity for profit arose. In the meantime, it simply amused him that they should be continuously vicious.

Alexander, the bigger of the two, seized the lead position every day as they set out, straining at the rope so determinedly that Martin allowed him his will rather than spend the day fighting to hold him in restraint. Julius, the smaller and more clever one, did not so much contest that lead openly but sought opportunities to humiliate his rival by suddenly replacing him there. When a variation of the terrain appeared that made arc to the right inevitable on the part of the pilgrims, the smaller horse anticipated it, made the loop earlier than the rest of the company, and suddenly appeared without effort in advance of his rival.

The big horse was then goaded to open fury by Julius's presence closer to the shimmering haunches of the lovely Dido just ahead. Relaxing on the rope, he would whip his great head and massive teeth to catch Martin and to end that restraint altogether. When the new groom foresaw the attack and sawed on the rope and the bit as savagely as he could to discourage it, the stallion would pull and rear, lashing out with one or the other iron-shod hoof. As this dangerous dance continued, Alexander would seize whatever momentary advantage he secured over his groom to let fly with his rear hooves against his competing suitor for the mare.

Rarely did he make even a glancing connection. Deliberately the smaller stallion would let the groom, Bertran, tug him out of range while squealing defiance. Eventually, with much raising of clouds of dust, jumbling of ox-carts, curses, ribald observations, and mounting laughter, the original order of the two stallions was resumed and relative peace returned to the procession.

No matter how often this little drama was repeated, the successful resolution of it depended almost entirely on the efforts of Martin. Leading the larger horse, he had to remain continuously alert to the chances for subtle aggression that their route opened up to the smaller horse. Bertran had refused the task of leading or attempting to control the big stallion. Even the smaller Julius dominated him easily when he chose. The young groom had been more ambitious once. His wily charge had turned on him then and had caught him by the side of the head with his hoof. As a result he had lost the eye and still bore a pronounced concavity on that side of his face. With the eye had gone whatever determination Bertran might once have had to control his charge.

Such equine passion exacted its costs from time to time. After making camp, Martin winced but held his left hand steady.

The pudgy priest was sure and deft as he bandaged the long, ragged tear that Alexander's teeth had made. The day's journey had been so peaceful on the whole that Martin had relaxed with the prospect of rest, and the great beast had seized its chance. Only the reflex born of much experience had saved him from the loss of a finger or worse. Simon had trimmed the ragged edges with a small knife and now was binding the whole with a tight bandage. Within it, against the wound itself, the priest had pressed some sort of moss which Martin did not recognize.

"He'll kill you, you know!"

"That horse? He'd like to, but I have dealt with animals all my life and it will be long before the brute gets such a chance again, Father."

"Not the horse, Martin. Not the horse. The real brute is the man. Some day Rainald will kill you. He will if you stay with the group. Why don't you just leave some night when we're all asleep? That devil would try to catch you but at least you'd have some chance that way. Here you have none."

The short priest was looking at him earnestly and Martin realized, with some surprise, that the older man had come to feel some responsibility for him.

"I could offer you the same advice, father. Rainald is no friend of yours either. And he has already killed your friend, the priest Gerald, whom you mentioned on my first day in this troupe."

"No," the other responded. "He isn't likely to kill me."

He hesitated and looked fixedly at the ground between them.

"I'm a coward. Rainald knows that and has no respect for me. That devil enjoys seeing me deny my own manhood bit by bit each day. He even lets me bury the dead and say my Mass for those of the group who have survived this long. His contempt extends to what I do as well as what I am. I'm no threat because I haven't the courage to resist him. Gerald tried that and was murdered for his trouble. The man only bothers to kill those who will fight. That's why you are in danger."

The silence that developed between them became awkward. The straightforward confidence of the little priest made him uncomfortable. It was like a confession and he knew its sincerity.

"Perhaps, but it is too late to make a run for it now. I've taken the responsibility for the woman, for Ermentrude. She couldn't possibly keep up if we made a dash for it. The knight would kill the both of us when he caught us and find pleasure in our having tried. But if I leave her behind and he doesn't succeed in catching me, he will kill her, probably slowly, surely terribly."

Simon looked long at the earnest features of the farmer. Loyal brown eyes, he thought. Serious brow. Not stupid but loyal. Will I shock him? Does that matter?

"It may be as you say, Martin. I would intercede for the woman but that might only make Rainald more determined to avenge himself on her. Still, have you thought that Ermentrude is not likely to live more than a month or two in any event? He won't let her drop out of the pilgrimage, even if she would. He won't let her find a place in one of the ox-carts. And if she keeps on walking, she is going to die from exhaustion. We've both seen the like before. It is as simple as that. You can't prevent that. I can't prevent it either. So why should you risk your life as well?"

"It may well be as you say, Father. She may die of weariness somewhere along the trail. People do. But still, other people do not. Sometimes the very ones we least expect to last do just that."

"Exactly! So the woman's fate is not in either of our hands. Maybe we can help her and maybe we can't, no matter what we do. So why not leave and I will do what I can for her? I could ask the woman herself what she would prefer—if you want me to do that. I myself think that she would tell you to go and let her take her own chances."

Even as he recognized the good intentions of the little priest, Martin was repelled by the suggestion. He knew his voice betrayed that.

"I would not ask her to make that decision. By itself, the question might kill her. God knows, she has little enough hope left as it is."

"And what is that to you? What kind of feeling do you have for her? That is the way one talks about a sister perhaps, or a wife. But you two do not share the same bed. I have watched ever since you championed her against Rainald. You do not even talk together overmuch."

It was no great admission the priest made. There was almost no privacy in the circumstances of the pilgrimage. The observation of the behavior of one another was, ordinarily, the sole amusement their circumstances afforded them. Mostly there was just the boredom of the road that promised to stretch out before them eternally. Since the farmer had first risked his life to save the woman, the presumption was that he would bed her and there were wagers made, changing sometimes daily, as to when that would finally happen. Thinking on it helped one and all forget the awful ache of their feet.

"I am not sure myself what I am doing or what I should do, Father. Perhaps she is part of my penance. Maybe it is God's joke that a woman should be my proper penance."

Simon had finished with the bandaging of the man's hand. He released it and regarded Martin soberly. The two sat somewhat apart from the rest and it was others' turns to set the fire and prepare the pot for the evening meal. After a minute Simon spoke.

"Am I supposed to guess what you mean by that? Or are you going to tell me?"

"No. I'll tell you. I married young. In a way I was lucky. Of my brothers or sisters I was the only one who lived for more than a year or two. When I was fourteen my mother died so there would be no more. My father, like most farmers, had married late and by that time had no taste to marry again. He was weary of most things by then. So the farm was to be mine anyway and he had no objection to my marrying so young. The new woman would keep the house, and make his pipe, and tend his aches.

"So it was that I found Claire. It was no great search. She lived in the village and I had known her since we were both children. But she was lovely—and even younger than I. When we wed she was but fifteen and I was only eighteen. She was as wild for me as I was for her. Sometimes in the summer she would come out to the fields for me. To bring me cool water, she said, but in truth it was so that we could share one another without my father looking on—or listening.

"But Claire was good to my dad, very good. He had no complaints of her. She was good about the garden and his clothes were always clean. When he took sick she nursed him night and day. He used to say that a father could get no better daughter.

"Still, in a dozen years she could not conceive. She would joke about it when she had helped with a sow's litter—or with the foaling of a calf. Yet it was her great sorrow. I used to think that it might be a punishment. I feared that our love was too ripe, too plentiful, too frequent. It seemed to me sometimes that I was always at her and that in my haste and passion, I gave her no chance to conceive. But she would not hear that. She swore that she had not married me to turn me into a monk. Then she would laugh and fold me into her arms. I never did really try to persuade her not to.

"Then, finally, Claire did find herself with child. But it was not right from the start. She wanted it to be right, as much as any woman ever wanted. But she was sick as no woman ever was, right from the beginning. It was as if she was carrying a demon instead of a baby. She got so pale and thin, so weak, that my old father began to care for her. I think that he had come to love her almost as much as I did. He did as much as he could by that time. Yet nothing helped—not herbs, not charms, not prayers. Had prayers any use at all, they would have saved Claire.

"She died in April. I was watching over her and she smiled. I turned away to get her a little soup and I heard a sigh. When I turned back she was gone. She simply slipped away like the spring breeze through the willow.

"For months I felt as though I was hollowed out inside. There was nothing there. I could work. And I did work—as long as the light lasted. Then I took care of my father. After Claire died, he wrapped himself in his bedroll and almost never moved from it. When I came in from the fields, I fed him and made him get up for a bit. Sometimes for no more than the time it took him to go out and empty his bowels. We were hermits, he and I. We never spoke of her but she had made the two of us closer than we had ever been in our whole lives. Now we just endured through each day together. It helped a little.

"How long had Therese been watching the two of us? Probably almost from the beginning. Our farm was not very rich but it was a solid place, long worked and the fields and fruit trees well established. We had only a few dairy cows but a good stud bull. Her own father had nothing but a hut falling down about his ears and the clothes on his back. For their keep he worked as shepherd, swineherd, whatever he could find. He had no land and was never going to have any. Our valley was modest and worked from ridge to ridge by families that had held their own for six, seven generations. He had come over the hill with a wife and an infant. No one knew him. He had no family there. He was scarcely able to find a wild place behind the church to build a hut.

"The wife died a year or so after they arrived. So there were no more kids. Therese grew mostly on her own. Her father collected wild berries and other sorts of fruits when he couldn't find any real work. He fermented a kind of drink from them that he could sometimes barter or sell to the poorer sort of family man. It didn't make him popular and he drank too much of it himself.

"And so his daughter saw the only opportunity she was ever going to have and she took it. I was stupid with sorrow and heedless of everything around me except for dad and the farm. She had just come into womanhood.

"Therese was fifteen when it began. Nothing had touched her. The cold, the hunger, the filth of her father's house—somehow the child had escaped it all. Now she was, for the moment, in full bloom. She had rich, lustrous black hair, coil after coil of it, and green eyes that looked out at you from under. Her voice was deep and her laugh rolled out of her throat in rhythms that made a man begin to sweat at the very hearing of it. Fine limbs she had, full-muscled but smooth and of a good length. She was tall for a village girl though not so tall as I myself. Firm breasts and buttocks too.

"In truth, considering what her childhood had been like, she was, just then, a sort of a miracle of nature. When she set her mind to win me I suppose there was never any doubt that she would succeed. The girl was bright. She knew the sorrow that ate at me. At the same time, she guessed as well that the emptiness in me longed to be filled by something, almost anything.

"Boldly she began to follow me about in the fields asking

me little girl questions about the oxen and the skills of plow-
ing. They did not fool me nor did she expect them to. It was a
sort of teasing. It was the kind of false indifference to his person that a woman practices in order to goad a man to parade
himself. I think that there was no real deceit between us from
the very start of it. She wanted the security of the farm desper-
ately and I knew that she wanted it. I wanted the warmth, the
comfort, the life that her body promised, and she understood
my terrible craving for her from the very beginning.

"At the same time I was haunted by the memory of Claire.
The presence of the girl, and my growing desire for her, made
my wife's memory yet more fresh. Every day that awful recol-
lection increased my guilt. Unless I could drive Therese away,
I knew that it could end only one way. But when I tried to
pretend anger at her the vixen retreated into her little girl imitation. She made her eyes big and watery and her breasts to
heave. She dropped back a few steps and followed me with
bowed head. But she never left. She knew that what troubled
me was my own lust and my guilt in feeling it.

"Soon enough I would look back, worried that she really
might lose interest and leave. Then she would smile as if the
heavens had just opened for her. In her rush to regain position
at my side she was sure to show her limbs and body to best
advantage. I was just as sure to catch sight of every bit of her
flesh that the opportunity offered. Again, we both were acting
a pretense and we both were aware of our own real intent and
of the other's understanding of it too. So the game went on,
growing more reckless every day.

"In her own fashion, a woman's fashion, Therese was deep.
She realized how dangerous the game was becoming. I think
that she feared that I might run away. It was possible. Either I
would do that or I might kill her because I so despised myself.
My guilt and my lust fed one another. She judged, finally, that

it was time to act and that no arguments from her could have a real effect on me.

"So she waited one morning until I was turning the plow team at the end of the furrow and I was fully occupied in the task. She stood on the verge of the field in the dappled sunlight of the trees and stripped herself of her ragged tunic. As she posed mutely there without moving, but with the play of light dancing on her body, I thought that my brain would burst. Perhaps it did.

"I forgot the oxen, the plow, the day itself. All that mattered was that I hold her body. Though I behaved like a bull in heat she made no resistance. Rather, she tore at my back and shoulders with her hands. She kissed my face, my eyes, my throat. She urged me on for as long as I was able. In our sudden passions we rolled off the verge itself and into the wet earth at end of the furrow. She began to laugh then, and laugh. I could hear her triumph in the sound but I did not care. I had found some terrible kind of release from the spell that had gripped me all through the past months. I shook with sobbing but I would not allow a sound to escape. We lay together there, in the wet mud of the furrow, and both of us celebrated the fulfillment of our desires.

"My father never accepted her. He would have disowned me but we had already been to the notary, he and I, and the farm was mine. I could bring Therese home and I did. We were married. The girl would have no less. Then her claim to the place was better than his and almost as good as mine.

"He never spoke to her. It was a strange thing. She was wildly happy and eager to please him if she could. But she was too ripe. She worked hard from the beginning and the garden plot and animals throve under her eye. Still, she could not hide that generous body of hers and my dad could see every passing minute what it was that had made me betray the memory of Claire. He despised me for that simple-minded, insatiable passion and he hated her.

"One day he disappeared. He just left, old and sick as he was. Sometime during the morning he slipped away and by night, when I came in from the field, he had not come back. It was a relief. My first thought was to make love with Therese. We didn't even stop to eat first. For all those months my father had been there, he didn't stop us from loving but his presence and his disapproval made it a little strained, awkward—less than abandoned. That night he was gone and I rejoiced in my desire.

"I told myself that I would look for him and bring him back in the morning. I didn't. He should have been easy to track. He was too sick to travel very far or very fast. But in my heart, I didn't want him back. He had become a living reproach to me—him and his silent witness to Claire. By God's blood, I remembered her well enough myself. I didn't need my father's condemnation every day. My own was enough for me.

"So I never looked. God forgive me! He must have made it out of the valley somehow. No one ever found his body and likely someone would have. It wasn't a big place. I was relieved at that too. It would have been a shame to me to have to bury him even. Everything was easier that he was just gone.

"Not that our life, Therese's and mine, was ever ordinary. My passion for her was constant, wild, and near savage. I gloried in her round and sweating nakedness. I had been avid enough with Claire, too much so maybe. But this was different still. There was excitement true enough—but hardly any sweetness in it. Sorrow drove me. Guilt too. I think I frightened Therese sometimes. She understood and so she never complained. She was an honest woman. She had bought me with her body and she would keep her bargain.

"While she had passion enough herself at times, it was the farm that delighted her. Why not? Therese had never had anything and now she had a house and a bed, a barn and animals, fruit trees and a piece of land that shone from the spring to the autumn. Now she was pregnant and she grew heavy and happy. But I was never able just to share that kind of happiness with her. I had the two deaths always with me. They drove me to her body but they kept me from sharing in the generosity of her soul.

"Then she too was taken. She and the child—but I didn't really care about the child. When I came in from the field I found them both. Somehow the bull had trapped her. Maybe just because she was heavy with child. Maybe because she had grown careless in her happiness. By the time that I found her she was stiff and cold. Even without those terrible wounds the grace had gone from her body. Now my own repulsion mocked me.

"I tied the bull fast to a tree and then I killed it with an axe. I went to see the priest and we buried the remains of Therese and the child in the churchyard next to Claire. The priest knew that I could not stay in the valley and so he suggested this pilgrimage. He did not want me in his parish. The neighbors did not want me in the village. They half believed that I would hang myself. It was possible. I was too dead for repentance. The word didn't mean anything at all to me. Escape was what I looked for.

"So I sold the farm for the money to travel. I began to walk and eventually I met your party outside of Jaca. Now I find myself with yet another woman. It is God's joke, not mine! Or maybe it is something much crueler than a joke."

Martin's voice trailed off. The bustle of the encampment became once again noticeable in the silence it left. Simon could think of nothing that should be said just now. The priest in him mentally rehearsed the words of absolution but his companion was not ready to hear them at this moment. There would be time enough for that. They had a long way yet to walk.

The two sat in the quiet for a bit. Then they rose and went their separate ways to find whatever was left to eat before the time to sleep should overtake the camp.

Chapter Five

They had camped well away from the pilgrim road in a small copse on the edge of rolling country. Ever since the route from the Somport Pass north of Jaca had joined with the other northern routes that crossed the Pyrenees at Roncesvalles north of Pamplona, the human throngs had more than tripled. Finding the road and campsites fouled with human and animal droppings, in disgust, Rainald had taken to locating their overnight camps well north of the thoroughfare. It meant a minor loss of time at the beginning and end of the day, but that was more tolerable than the trailside filth.

Martin woke suddenly. Some obscure shift of shadow warned him. He half-rolled to his right. The knife drove narrowly past his neck into the partially exposed tree root cushioned with his overtunic. But his assailant was carried on top of the farmer by the force of his drive and he pushed Martin back to earth. The man was heavy and Martin could get no leverage.

Martin grasped the right arm of the attacker as conciousness returned with a rush. In a second he realized that the man's weapon was fouled somehow. Martin pulled the knife arm to spoil the other's attempt to clear it. In return, his enemy clasped him tightly about the body. That grip, combined with the stranger's greater weight, pinned Martin against the ground. Over their grunting in the dark, the farmer could hear one of the stallions screaming.

Vainly scrabbling for purchase he realized that the man was going to kill him as soon as he was able to free the knife. But now his opponent's weight shifted suddenly to Martin's left and the latter was able to get his right leg braced against the ground and roll his attacker under him.

"Kill him, Martin, kill him!"

Ermentrude! It was Ermentrude! She held the man's left leg and continued to hold it against the attacker's frenzied kicking. The woman had used her grip to shift the attacker's weight just enough to give the farmer his advantage.

The intruder still struggled to free his knife but now he had only his forearm for leverage. Then the sword flashed across the farmer's vision. The attacker's wrist erupted in blood as the hand hung free, severed cleanly. Martin started back from the sight and the screams that followed. Once more the sword gleamed dully before Martin's eyes and bit into the man's throat. While the man under him choked in near silence, the screams of the stallion continued to fill the night.

"Come on, farmer! There's more work over there."

Rainald stood an instant, sword dripping blood, barefoot and clothed only in a short tunic, before bounding off in the direction of the stallions. Heaving himself up from the new corpse beneath him, Martin snatched his own knife and followed on the run.

Emerging from a large cloudbank, the moon cast sudden illumination on the scene just before the two. The stallion Alexander trampled a battered and sodden heap methodically under his front hooves. A large rag that had been used to blindfold him hung loosely about the big horse's neck. It must have slipped free just as his would-be kidnapper had loosened the hobble securing the stallion for the night. That piece of carelessness had proved fatal and the huge animal screamed his defiance still. A few feet away, the smaller of the two horses, Julius, stood quiet but trembling. A makeshift hood covered his head but his hobble was secure.

Some yards off, under a tall pine, a bundle of bedding was tossed and tangled. Martin had little doubt of what it concealed but he advanced to examine it. His quick twitch of one edge of the mass brought into the pale moonlight the sight of his fellow groom, Bertran. The man's single, good eye glared upward as if to protest the blood oozing from his nose and mouth. He had been taken suddenly and unprepared. There was nothing to be done for the murdered groom.

Martin could see that the knight Rainald had led the bigger stallion away from the bloody mess under his hooves. Now he was gentling the horse, soothing him with quiet words half-crooned. At the same time, his iron grip upon the halter rope was preparing the stallion to be hobbled securely once more. Despite himself, the one-time farmer was impressed by the man's mastery of the beast and the calm with which he had taken control of the situation. Martin approached the smaller of the horses and began to sing quietly to him, while stroking the beast's neck and shoulders. Ever so gradually the muscle tremors subsided and finally he was able to remove the blindfold from the terrified Julius. Then he closely examined its hobble to make sure that it still secured the animal.

By this time the remainder of the knight's retinue had pounded up. The five of them stood about, half armed and half clothed, unsure of what was expected of them.

"Do you want us to start a search for them, lord?" the eldest of the group, Stephen, finally ventured.

"Search where, you dolt? The bunch of you just managed to get lost in your own camp—if I'm not mistaken. Or did you hang back intentionally, hoping to see me knifed, so that you could appropriate my goods and treasures? Or was it that you had no stomach for close quarters at night with a band of hill bandits?

"No matter. They're well away from here by now and we'd never find them in the dark.

"Go back to your slumbers for now. In the morning we'll find the bastards and teach them better than to make attempts on the property of a gentleman. You too, farmer. I'll want you along in the morning. We may need some of your special gifts if I choose to interrogate some of these brigands before I send them to that hell where they belong. But make sure that horse is well tethered before you sleep. Sleep here, although I don't think that our visitors will return. They doubtless think that they have had grief enough though I shall see that they have more and plenty.

"Pull dear Bertran's carcass off into the wood a little way. He'll be bad company and worse smell shortly. His burial can be seen to in the morning by your priest friend."

This last came over the knight's shoulder as he moved off into the wood in the direction of the main camp. His men-at-arms followed him uncertainly and Martin was left alone with the stallions and the dead groom.

The sun was just up. Rainald already had gathered about him his men-at-arms when Martin joined them, answering the summons of the knight.

"Now that we're all assembled, I'll want you two," pointing to the oldest two of his men, "to remain here in control of the pilgrims. Nothing is to be undertaken until I return. Is that clear? Nothing at all. No one leaves this camp before then. Those who are impatient can busy themselves with the repair of the carts and the tackle. Look to it."

The two men moved off—not displeased to be left out of what promised to be a hard march at the very least, but trying with not too much success to hide their relief. Their master watched them go with undisguised contempt. After a moment, he turned toward the others.

"The rest of you are going to have a quick march this morning. I calculate that we can overtake our attackers of last night sometime about noon or perhaps a bit before. There can't have been more than a dozen of them to begin, I think. Two were killed here so that the odds will be more in our favor. Their arms will be old stuff—loot from murdered pilgrims probably. You have the good weapons I have supplied and you are trained to their use by me, as those bandits have not been. It should be a slaughter. And that's if they dare to put up a fight. More likely they'll run as if the very devil pursued them at the first sight of me, mounted on Julius here. But I won't expect you to let them get away—any of them. Whatever you find on the ones that you kill, you can keep. I just want that rabble's leader."

No one else seemed willing to put voice to the question, so Martin did.

"Your pardon, my lord, but can we hope to catch them on their own ground? And them with a long lead and us only guessing which way they will have fled?"

"So now you are a tactician, eh, farmer? Leave the plans to someone who understands the matter. In the first place, they will have no more than an hour's lead. They are not likely to have blundered about the countryside in the dark any more than we. No one wants a broken ankle or a sharp branch in the eye. And since we didn't pursue them at all last night, they'll be pretty sure that we won't this morning. They're on the move now, but not too rapidly for us to catch them before they come to understand with whom they're dealing.

"In the second place, this is no more their country than it is ours. The local people here make the best part of their living off virtuous pilgrims like ourselves. They'll be no friends of robber scum and more apt to betray them than to hide them—if given the chance. No, my guess is that they'll have come from beyond that range of hills you can see to the north there. Now they will head back to the safety of their own lands through that gap you can make out just off to the left—where I'm pointing. But we'll have a little surprise for them well before they get to it.

"Now a question for you, rustic. Can you handle a war bow?"

At a motion from the knight, one of his retainers thrust a bow and quiver at Martin.

"I have often used a bow for hunting, my lord."

Rainald regarded him for a long moment.

"Try to remember that this bow throws a heavy arrow farther than your hunting bow did. Then too, you won't be any good up close to our bandits. They are more practised in the use of a knife than you are. They'd have very little trouble gutting you. Just hang behind the rest of my brave men here and take a shot at any target you think that you can hit. Especially if any one of them happens to have a bow too. Even if you can't hit them, you can spoil their aim."

Without further words, the knight neck-reined Julius away and started the stallion out at the smart pace he was to maintain through the morning. For the quartet of men following in his track on foot they found themselves moving at a slow trot from the very beginning. Before they had gone half a mile from camp they were all drenched with sweat and breathing hoarsely. But no one slowed or wasted breath on complaints.

The relaxed posture of Rainald made clear his expectation that they would be in sight if he should turn to summon or direct them.

The country was rough and becoming rougher as they hurried north. The forest was mostly pin oak and fir with considerable scrub. Where Julius had not broken or trampled it in his passage, it caught the arms and clothing of the men on foot and whipped against their legs. As best they could, they followed, one after the other. By now, the best and the youngest of them were almost at the point of exhaustion. Sweat burned in their eyes and their mouths were dry. The distance between them and Rainald had lengthened but still the knight continued, imperturbable, in his pace. Only the fear by which he held them kept them in pursuit.

Then, up ahead on the brink of a small knoll, the knight reined in abruptly and awaited them in some impatience. At the prospect of a full halt, they all pushed their aching legs harder and managed to gather around their master before his visage had become too black.

"We've caught up with our quarry. I have had them in sight for a little while now. They have not yet seen me so their gait is very leisurely. Now we'll abandon any pretense of care and launch a full pursuit. When we do, they'll take to their heels in earnest. But there's a clearing down below that they have to cross. We have to take them before they reach its far side. That way Julius and I will have full freedom to manuever.

"Spread out now. Keep three horse-lengths between you. I doubt that they'll have enough good sense to form a line or to try to slip around us. Surprise is the best weapon against brigands like these. Still, I don't want anyone behind us with time to string a bow.

"Smartly now. Earn your loot or, by God, I'll make you wish you never left your mothers' teats."

The warrior wheeled his mount and signaled his intent to the stallion with a sharp slap to its withers. Julius responded instantly and as he bounded forward, Rainald first stood in the stirrups for a moment and unsheathed his sword in one, long, smooth motion. Then he settled over the animal's neck, trusting it to avoid any overhanging branch stout enough to do either of them damage.

Behind him the four men spread out as they ran behind him. The excitement of impending battle was so strong in them that their fatigue drained away in an instant. Each was busy with the search, moment by moment, for a safe place to plant the next foot. In the scrub they could see no one and the only sound, beyond their own laboring breath, was the crash of the stallion, now a bow shot ahead. The robbers could not help but hear this too.

Up ahead a confusion of shouting broke out. At their distance, Martin and his fellows could make no sense of it. Plunging forward still, they began now to glance from side to side, anxious to catch sight of the enemy before they should be surprised by some sudden encounter. But no foe appeared and in an instant more, they had reached the edge of the clearing of which Rainald had spoken.

The bandits had given no thought to a fight. As one man they had taken to their heels at the first sight of the horseman pursuing them, his blond hair flowing in the wind, sword extended, and horse at full gallop. The fleetest pair of them were already within bow shot of the trees on the far side of the glade. A half dozen others were strung out behind the leaders. Rainald was now almost within a spear cast of the laggards and was closing on them fast.

Martin and the men-at-arms slowed to a halt at the edge of the meadow. Weary as they were, there remained little chance that they could overtake their now alerted and fresher antagonists once the latter had reached the tree line on its far side. Nor were they anxious to catch them, now that the first excitement of battle had cooled. On the slight possibility that additional members of the bandit gang had taken cover in the long meadow grass, they now began to beat forward slowly, keeping their line extended as a precaution. Martin had his bow at the ready with war arrow nocked but he did not believe that any of those panicky figures hastily rushing toward the shadows of the far edge of the clearing was likely to halt there and begin cover fire for his fellows behind.

The real interest of the knight's footmen soon focused upon the drama now beginning near the center of the field. There, a great bear of a man clad partially in the skin of that same animal and carrying a spiked war club as thick as a man's biceps halted to make a stand. The others streamed past him, eager to gain the safety of the far tree line. He shouted something to them in a strange tongue but they paid no heed. Perhaps he called on them to rally about him or may have encouraged them to find some good place to make a stand. For certain, none of the bandits knew how many their pursuers numbered. Not just one, half-armed knight, for sure!

Now Rainald was almost upon the burly figure, who launched his club in a long, low arc designed to take Julius at the knees and bring down horse and rider. At the last possible moment the stallion responded from long habit to the slight pressure of his master's right knee and swerved just far enough to avoid the intended blow. Simultaneously, the horseman leaned far to his right and swept his sword down in a long, clean backstroke. For a moment none of his supporters could tell for sure whether the knight had found his target.

Then, as Rainald reined up his steed well beyond his prey, they could see that the heavy man had dropped his war club and was attempting to use his left hand to staunch the spurt of blood from the lower part of his right arm. The knight appreciated the condition of his enemy at once and had already begun to guide his stallion in a slow, prancing approach toward the bandit leader. The man stood his ground, trying to find some way to repair his wound. At the same time, he regarded the aproaching knight dumbly, unsure of what to expect but making no move to run or to defend himself.

The blond horseman drew slowly up to this still figure, and extended his sword arm until the weapon's tip was just touching the man's throat. The bandit did not flinch nor did he attempt to speak. His eyes held those of the knight's. Ever so gradually, Rainald drew back the blade, while he directed a slow smile towards his victim. Then, with the speed of a striking snake, he drove the blade deep into the man's left biceps and wheeled away.

Behind him, the man staggered, but then regained a sort of balance. In his confusion, he attempted to grasp his biceps with his already useless right hand. Then, giving up that futile endeavor, he readied himself for death without even the slightest effort to flee. His nemesis, meanwhile, wheeled his horse back and forth in silence at some little remove.

The stallion was excited with the lust of blood and neighed violently, cavorting just under control of the tightest of reins. Martin and the others were transfixed with the scene before them. The farmer noted, in some corner of his mind, the brilliant green of the grass in the golden sun, and the red of the blood running down into it. Distant bird sounds only accented the silence in the meadow.

Then, all of a sudden, Rainald began to laugh. The high-pitched sound was mirthless. He launched his mount into motion then, coming near to full gallop as he bore down on the wounded figure there. The sword came back, then forward, for a sweeping stroke. But at the last possible moment the knight again guided the horse away, so that the tip of the blade just flashed along the side of the man's head, opening a long wound, from which the blood began immediately to course down into the right eye and along the whole side of his face.

Once more there was a pause as the excited stallion was guided in tight circles about the stricken bandit chieftain. Half-blinded, and welling blood from his three different wounds, the man could make no effort, even so much as to follow the movements of his persecutor. From the blind right side, Rainald again flashed by his victim and, in his passage, opened up a long wound across the man's chest, severing the bearskin coat and undertunic but stopping just short of penetrating the ribcage.

Now the knight wheeled his mount, time and again, in full view of the bandit chief. As he did so, he rose in the stirrups and swung his sword in a dazzling display of perfect balance and control. Gradually he eased his mount closer while sawing on its bit. Julius responded by pawing the air with his front hooves just beyond the weaving figure while he screamed frantically and danced on his rear legs. Always the sword glinted in the sunlight and flashed about the bloodied chieftain.

Then, without another blow, the man's nerve broke. He began to scream shrilly. The sounds made no words in any language but were of fear and pain. Martin and the others were sure of that. While the hair on their bodies prickled and their guts tightened, the awful terror continued to find voice.

Rainald himself drew off just the smallest distance. He sat for long moments listening to the animal lament issuing from the bloodied creature. He smiled. The tight, controlled tension of the champion in battle drained from his body. Slowly, almost languidly, he walked his stallion around that stupefied creature. So quickly that the eye scarcely registered the movement, he swung the heavy sword in a final, backhand movement. Its edge caught the unfortunate victim full in the throat, silencing his screams. The head dropped back and just failed to part from the body, still connected by its stalk. The heavy body shuddered and sank into the grass.

No one spoke. No one moved. Even Julius was quiet.

Three quarters of the way across the field there was a flash of rags in motion. A single bandit had gone to earth there unnoticed and had, till now, been held fascinated amidst the grass by the terrible drama just concluded. He bolted, running head down and body well forward to make the smallest target.

Martin held the only strung bow in the band and he stepped to one side from the others to get a clear sighting. There would be time for but one shot.

"Let him go, farmer."

Rainald's voice carried clear from where he sat watching.

"He'll have a pretty tale to tell the others. Something to make their guts twist and their bowels run loose. It will make the pilgrimage trail about these parts safer for a month or two at any rate. Nor would you likely hit him with a new bow, and a good arrow would be lost."

"Justice has been served. Leave this carrion for the wolves and the crows as a reminder of that. Now all you brave fellows, get yourselves back as swift as you can. We can at least make a few miles before the day is out."

So saying, the knight urged his horse into the scrub and was soon lost to their view. To a man, they were glad of his absence.

Chapter Six

"Sit there! On the log, farmer! Even dry wood is softer to the buttocks than the earth of this parched and blasted land. Only religion could have made me come here from the sweetness of my native soil. Whom the Gods will destroy, they first make mad, eh?"

Martin sat as he had been bid. The summons of the knight had been unexpected and issued without explanation, as was the man's custom. It had come as he was sitting before the fire, after having eaten the day's meal. Now Martin sat before the blaze prepared apart each evening by one of Rainald's men-at-arms, Luke. Ever since the pilgrims had descended from the low mountains west of the River Ebro and had emerged on the great plain, a night fire was hardly necessary for warmth. But it was a comfort nonetheless. Pilgrims and knight alike kept the cook-fire going long into the evening, well after it had served its prime purpose.

"I am surprised, farmer, that you have neglected to take the Flemish woman into your bed. Your reluctance makes me wonder whether you have taken some sort of monkish vow for your sins or whether you are just one of those sodomites who would mate with man or sheep before they would touch a mere woman. Surely you are still too young to have lost all taste for things soft and round and wet. Do I wrong you?"

"But, my lord, you yourself warned me, when I became your ostler as warrant and blood-price for the woman, that I was not to presume that her virginity was forfeit to me thereby."

"Come now, come now, Martin, do not play the fool with me. I have watched you, off and on, these past weeks and seen that you have no small share of brains—for a farmer born. You handle my lovely horses better than ever did that boob, Robert, before your lady killed him. A poetic end for the lout, by the way. You were alone among my men in that little encounter with the bandits who showed any great presence of mind.

"So don't expect me to tolerate your playing at mock obedience to explain why you should refrain from a perfectly ordinary use of the woman. You understand well, I warrant, that such a lapse on your part would have amused me greatly. I would have savored your indulgence on the doubtless dry and hard body of that aging crone. The thought of you trying to find pleasure in thrusting yourself into that dusty treasure box would have entertained me for weeks. Perhaps that is exactly why you refrained? Do you set yourself up to thwart me at every turn?"

The words were delivered in a gentle tone, but the menace that underlay them was clear. How did one answer such apparent banter? It was not lost on Martin that, for the first time, the knight had addressed him by his Christian name. Martin knew that any assumption of greater familiarity on his part would be furiously resented. He could not take a corresponding lightness of tone in his reply—for he had already been warned against it. Neither could he respond to the implicit invitation of the other to account for his abstinence by a further denigration of the woman herself. However luckless and plain the Flemish Ermentrude might be, he was prevented by a certain pity from taking advantage of her misfortunes to escape his own. There was, also, some resentment he felt at being called to account by this vicious young man. Under the circumstances, the only escape might lie in some slight revelation of himself.

"Pardon, lord. I do not dream of opposing your wishes. I am hardly so foolish as to court suicide. The matter is simply this: in a short three years, I have buried two wives. That is why I find myself a pilgrim on his way to the shrine of Saint James. The hurt is in part, not just that I have lost them, but that in some measure, the fault in their deaths is mine. The sadness I carry makes me indifferent to women's charms for the first time in my life."

Rainald was silent for just a bit. The mask that was his face remained composed. Martin nevertheless wondered if the man were not genuinely confused. That would be the first such case in all the time which he had known the young noble. Finally, the familiar, sardonic smile reappeared.

"By God, Martin, I think that you may be an honest man. May God forgive you for it. No one else ever will, I assure you. Certainly, I won't.

"I will end by killing you. I have always abhorred honest men. They are so pleased with themselves. They are so convinced of their own honesty—their righteousness. Usually they are dull things, although I confess that I sometimes find you interesting. Usually such people have just one virtue, just one talent, and they busy themselves endlessly with the practice of it. It is enough to drive a cheerful sinner like myself mad. I'm sure that it more than excuses the poor wretch who is forced to murder them.

"I do intend to kill you, you know. In my own good time I will kill you. You have set yourself up as my judge with your silent looks and your damned abstinence against my wishes.

For the time you are safe, for you are a good groom to my beautiful steeds. Alexander may even have gotten fond of you. But Alexander is the stupid one. Julius is more like me. He keeps his own counsel and loves no one. Watch yourself with Julius. All the same, when it becomes more convenient, I shall kill you. You believe me, don't you?"

"Yes, my lord, I do believe that you plan to kill me."

"That I 'plan' to kill you. You miserable creature! You contradict me again. When I decide to kill you, I will do just that. It will happen. Make no mistake. Why don't you run away some night?"

"Because I think that you would catch me, my lord."

Rainald smiled pleasantly. He sat for a space eyeing his groom.

"Oh yes. I likely would catch you. I'm quite good at tracking. You have seen that. But even if I did not, I have a hostage who would die most dreadfully in your place. So you can't even try to escape, can you?"

"You mean Ermentrude, I think."

"Just so, Martin, just so. I know, and you know, that there is more to this business between the Flemish ogre and yourself than you care to admit. You are a bright man for a farmer, yet you have accepted the burden of her. For some reason you have also come to see yourself as the protector of the priest, Simon. You joined us when my quarrel with him was already established. Yet you dared to befriend him. Perhaps I have two hostages for your surly service. Martin, dear Martin, you are a consummate fool!"

The other felt a chill, not at the threat which he had already accepted, but at the extent to which the man understood him. That knowledge of his unvoiced feelings left him somehow more helpless in the face of his persecutor. He felt that this line of interrogation could only become more ugly.

"Your lordship called me here. Was there some question about the stallions? They are both healthy. I am proud of that, for they are both beautiful animals and I should be sorry if they had suffered because of my failings."

"Beautiful, Martin. I have frightened you with all this unnecessary talk about killing and so you wish to turn our little talk to safer topics. Such tact! Very well. The horses are content and healthy. That is your doing, largely, and so you discharge the bound service that you owe me. That is just, and your noble soul must revel in that knowledge.

"You may even make me rich. Would that please you—that I should be indebted to you in some tiny respect? I shall sell my sword here, perhaps to this King Alfonso whom everyone thinks is such a great warrior. Peasants! What do they know of warriors and their ways?

"Yes, I shall sell it at a very good price and the stallions are essential to my appearance and my equipment. They mark me for a great man to the stupid. And most men are stupid, are they not, Martin?

"But these horses will enrich me with their very seed, as well. Most of the horseflesh that I have seen here is undersized. Good enough, in its way, but too small for really serious fighting. Alexander and Julius, put to stud, will make me wealthy while they pleasure themselves and bolster the cause of the cross against the heathen in this land. All this costs me nothing. It overjoys them. You may become famous, Martin— a very patron saint of grooms. Death enobles, you know."

"I am grateful if my service to you gains me some little time yet, lord."

The admission cost him nothing. It was literally true. While he could not see how he might avoid eventually being murdered by the man, Martin was young enough still to be happy that such a prospect was not too immediate.

"But I am puzzled that you should have joined a pilgrimage when you had a more magnificent prospect beckoning. I am here in penitence, however things may turn out. That is what makes pilgrims. But you certainly had no need for this band, or for its purpose, I think, yet you chose to become its leader."

"I 'chose' to become its leader! How delicately you put it. Is that what our dear Simon told you? Never mind. You add curiosity about me to your other impertinences. However, it is a long trip, this pilgrimage, and we have time to entertain even such temerity as your own.

"Like you, I am a pilgrim. Before I set about becoming rich and famous, I shall make my way to Compostela and Saint James. I have a penance of my own to perform."

Here Rainald hesitated for a long moment. Then his eyes lit up and he leaned forward, just slightly, and lowered his voice significantly. He became the very image of a man imparting a confidence.

"Would you believe that I am a thief? The stallions are not mine but my brother's. Well, they were my brother's. Does that surprise you?"

Martin had no thought to answer the query. At this particular moment, any response was dangerous. So too was no response—but he chose that course. His silence seemed to exasperate the knight.

"Don't worry so much, Martin. Do you indeed think that the reaction of a country bumpkin like yourself matters to me? I only tell you these things to further your education—to teach you something of the world of the great. I am enlarging your life, Martin. Listen closely. It can't hurt you, and you are a dead man in any case.

"I killed my brother and stole—well, took—his stallions. He was an older brother. Older brothers are a burden, at best. But dear Ralph was so more than most. He was like you, in some respects. Honest he was—and dull—and pleased with himself. Oh he was very pleased with himself. He positively basked in his own virtue.

"And my father took him at his own evaluation. My father doted on his oldest son. Not that that's unusual. All younger sons expect that. But father loved me as well. I'm sure of it. After all, he forgave me. Well, he let me leave in peace anyway.

"But my father loved Ralph too greatly—and I therefore found my brother a great nuisance. He was heir. He patronized me. Him! He was actually kind to me, when he had thought for me at all. Yes, he thought himself a very paragon of virtue.

"It was no great trick, finally, to goad him into a rage. He was sure that I had wronged him; misjudged him. He demanded an apology and of course I refused. I suggested that he must recoup his honor in a sword fight to the first blood. The dolt actually fancied himself a swordsman!

"So he became the challenger. We had to keep the match a secret from father; but the rest was easy. He was as simple to kill as that great oaf of a bandit the other week. But, of course, it had to appear more like an accident. Everyone had to appreciate that it was a stroke too vigorous, given in the heat of the encounter. Sad. So terribly sad.

"Afterward, father was heartbroken. But then, he was fair. Ralph had caused his own death, after all. My blow was intended only as a scratch. Even so, the old fellow could no longer abide the sight of me. Or of the stallions of my brother! I suggested a pilgrimage to remove the lot of us from his presence and to satisfy for my sin and he fell in with it gladly.

"But you and I know better, don't we Martin? You find yourself in the company of a true monster."

Rainald stopped and peered closely at Martin. The sounds of the night filled the silence between them. Somewhere an owl was stirring. The hunters were awakening. The long howl of the wolf echoed afar. There would be blood aplenty on the leaves before the moon was up.

Martin considered what he might say. Clearly he was expected to respond to this most extraordinary tale. In some measure, it had been told him just to elicit some reaction. Rainald insisted that his feelings were of no import but the farmer suspected that that was only partially true. More than anyone else in the pilgrim band, the knight was alone. Except for the occasional native woman who slunk into the camp at night, he had no companions. The man needed a priest. He needed to be shriven of his guilt. Perhaps that was the reason, or part of it anyway, why he had killed Gerald and daily humiliated Simon. Now he confesses himself to me, thought Martin.

"I think, my lord, that you give yourself little, or no, credit at all in such a terrible matter. Surely you must have been provoked—even if your deed was extreme."

His careful reply infuriated the knight. The man's voice came slightly raised, almost bereft of its ordinary tight control.

"You are a damned hypocrite, my friend. You maneuver to save your own skin by making excuses for what I have done that neither you nor I can believe. You treat me as though I were a coward. I know what I am and I do not require the sanctimonious sympathy of rustics. Christ, you should have been a priest! You would be rich by now—you and your careful tiptoeing about the filth of the world.

"Well, you will not escape me. I offer you a confidence and you hike up your skirts like a woman walking around turds. You purse your lips and mumble safe lies. But I will rub your nose in shit and see what you do then."

Rainald visibly drew back and sucked in great mouthfuls of air. He fell silent for a little. Gradually the old, sardonic smile reappeared. He was again in full control of himself.

"We seemed to have talked of many things, my dear Martin, even if your part in our little conversation has been deeply disappointing. However, I only called you here to expand your responsibilities. Did not the Lord Himself say that 'he who is faithful in small things shall be set over many?'

"I have told you already that I have been pleased with the way in which you have cared for my horses. I also noted that you were quick to accept what had to be done in our little skirmish of the other week. I trust that you have practised enough with the bow that I gave you to cut something of the figure of a man-at-arms by now.

"You need to be that, for I am putting you in charge of this company of pilgrims whenever I must be absent. In the coming weeks, increasingly I will have to scout and politic as we move along, and that sort of business will take me away from the camp for days at a time. I will expect you to keep the band moving and to maintain good order while I am absent.

"It is a task worthy of your talents. My other men-at-arms are brutes enough to cow our reluctant companions, but I mistrust their ability to lead. They would create more troubles than they would solve. They have been told that I am putting you in charge of them—as well as the rest. They don't like it but they accept it out of their fear of me.

"So watch your back at night, dear friend. No one is so hated in this world as those who rise in it. The weak are doubly pitiable because they are so filled with jealously of their betters. These men of mine will not dare to do anything openly, but you could have an accident. I would hate to be robbed of my own future pleasure by such churls.

"You are beginning now to see how you are going to serve

me? You think yourself my better. You dare to sit in judgment on me mentally. But I intend to prove to you that you will do anything I ask in order to save your own miserable life—and with it that of the woman and the priest. To keep yourself and them alive, you are going to help me become rich. You are going to be my instrument in commanding this pilgrimage.

"Do you think it likely that your friend Simon will forgive you that? But it may be that the woman will be impressed by your newfound greatness. Take your consolations where you may, my good friend, because I am going to make you come to hate yourself. You may yet come to shudder at the evils you will do in my name.

"And when you have come to loathe and despise yourself, I shall kill you, but only after I kill Simon and the Flemish woman. You see, I want you to understand that all the vices you will have come to practice still will not preserve their miserable lives. Before you yourself perish, I will demonstrate to you the futility of your little compromises with evil and your own essential rottenness.

"But don't lose hope, Martin. So long as you still hope, you are my prisoner and my most faithful servant. Hope is what makes for the best of servants and a man cannot have too many such. When you lose hope, then it is that you cease to be trustworthy and your friends will die. So, sleep soundly, my friend. On the morrow your duties will have greatly increased."

The knight made a small gesture of dismissal.

Chapter Seven

Simon winced and pulled back a little, as he had more than once since the big Fleming had begun her ministrations. In its careless unloading, the cooking tripod had slipped from his grasp and one of its legs had torn a long, irregular gash in his own. It was not terribly deep but some skin hung in a narrow flap and the whole had been dirtied in his surprised reaction. There had been nothing for it but to clean the wound, to sew its edges, and to bind the whole tight.

Since no one else had shown much enthusiasm for the task, Ermentrude had volunteered to carry it through. Quickly it had become clear to Martin that the nature of the ugly tear strained what knowledge of home remedies the woman possessed. She had collected the herbs for the dressing fast enough and they now lay by, ready for their final application. But the size of her hands made the plying of the needle difficult and she held the priest's shin immobile with a grip that would have steadied the stoutest plow.

Simon had not complained audibly, but he, like the woman, was sweating profusely. Both patient and makeshift physician clearly had doubts about what was being done but there was no help for it. Martin offered the priest another swallow from the wineskin and Ermentrude ceased her sewing for the moment. She did not, however, relax her hold on the offending leg. The limb seemed determined to thwart her and she would not have been surprised to see it attempt to walk off half-mended. Its little owner swallowed, sighed almost inaudibly, and again submitted to her attentions.

Finally it was done and the leg bandaged. Martin once more passed the skin to the priest who took it eagerly and held it long. There was a pallor beneath the smooth brown surface of his face. The farmer smiled in encouragement to Ermentrude, who watched the two men impassively.

"I suppose you think that you could have done better?"

He was dumbfounded by the outburst and the bitterness of the tone in which it was delivered. He had said nothing—offered no criticism, or even comment—while the operation had been in progress. It was true that he had not offered to help. But then, he knew little of this sort of medicine himself.

"No, no, I don't know much about treating wounds like that. No one else here does either."

"Including me, you mean. Well, I didn't see any of your friends offering to do the dirty job."

The woman was furious now. Her face, which had been pale and strained as she had worked, was suddenly flushed. He could see a vein pulsing in her forehead and her eyes glittered wetly.

"I didn't say that. I just meant that you did better than anyone else here could have—man or woman. You did fine. Simon would agree to that too. Wouldn't you, Simon?"

The priest was less than happy to be included in what was rapidly becoming a personal quarrel between the man and woman, if he was any judge of such things. His leg ached and he was feeling sleepy from the wine. He wanted no part of what seemed to be developing here. Still, Martin was his friend.

"I think you did a good job too, Ermentrude."

The woman glanced at him with something approaching contempt. Then she turned her wrath again to Martin.

"You think that I am a stupid woman, don't you? You feel sorry for me! Poor Ermentrude! So clumsy! So plain! It's a pity that she ever left her farmyard. We have to take care of her for she has no one."

She had lost her usual taciturn manner now. Her voice was suddenly shrill, elevated, close to breaking. The pilgrims who stood within earshot were grinning and some of them snickered. They were enjoying the unexpected attack of this old virago on the former farmer who had been so strangely chosen by the knight to be trail leader of the pilgrimage. Then too, all of them had at least once been set upon by some village woman for reasons that they never understood. It was a familiar comedy and they were enjoying Martin's evident bewilderment.

"Well, you are the stupid one, farmer. Did ever you wonder that poor Ermentrude was so happily on hand to save your miserable life that night when the robbers attacked? What did you think that she was doing there in the middle of the night? Going out to piddle in the dark, perhaps? No, you arrogant bastard. You probably never thought about it at all. You just assume that God has you in His special care. You are so dear to Him!"

His head bent under this storm of words. Martin realized with a start that he had not thanked the woman for her help. The action of Rainald had been decisive. The events that followed had so shocked him, had so occupied him, that the Fleming's earlier part in it had passed right out of his mind. Guiltily now, he pulled a little more back into himself as the angry flow of words continued.

"You were so proud of your generosity. You, the brave one, who bearded the knight to save my miserable life. Everyone saw it! Everyone one of these gaping fools standing around us now expected that you would claim your reward by taking me to bed. After all, that is the way of men with women they have rescued, isn't it?

"And you ignored me! You humiliated me in front of them all. You acted as though I were some poor cow you had pulled out of a marsh—to be set out to pasture in safety and quiet. I was too poor a thing—me with my big feet, my big hands, my old body—even to arouse your manly lust! You preferred even your lonely bed to me!"

She was on her feet now. She stood in front of him, bending over him slightly. Ermentrude had lost all control and her body shook like one with a fever. Her voice approached a shriek.

"Well, I'll tell you how I happened to be there to save your worthless life. I was trying to creep into your bed. I was going to throw myself—to force myself—on you. I was going to make you acknowledge me as your woman so that I could hold my head up amidst the snickers of these louts who travel with us.

"That was how I came to save you from that murdering thief. Fool that you are, what you never knew until now was that robber saved you from me! He gave his life for your precious virtue!"

She was sobbing now. Unsteadily she turned and half-trotted into the surrounding wood.

Martin was paralyzed. His surprise at the woman's avowals was total. She had been an embarassment to him ever since his offer to stand surety for her with Rainald. After Claire, after Therese, he had no present desire for women, any woman. He had borne the mocking innuendo of the knight, for the man did not understand, did not care to understand. But he simply had not thought that the woman might feel her position so keenly and take it as personal rejection. He had not even dreamed of trying to explain his past or his feelings to her.

Simon the priest had been unwilling witness to all of the scene and sat still, his back against the cartwheel. Now he pulled himself upright, favoring his throbbing leg. He smiled wryly at his friend.

"So now you see, Martin, why some of us count ourselves happy to take refuge in the priesthood. There are days when being able to plead that one has forsaken the flesh is a positive comfort. Three things a man can never understand—God, the Devil, and women!"

Laboriously Simon made his way along the side of the cart and then disappeared behind it.

Martin sat, not looking up, while all about him the amusement of the onlookers gradually gave way to hunger. In small groups they ladled themselves bits and pieces of stew from the cookpot and sought out some more or less comfortable spot to eat, still grumbling at one another over their portions. The lucky ones produced a bit of hard bread from somewhere on their persons to soften in the mysterious juices of their stew bowl.

Usually that ritual was leisurely and comfortable after another tiring day on the pilgrim road. But tonight there was an urgency and haste to finish the meal. Tonight was midsummer eve and there was an expectation and excitement in all their manners.

Soon, in the lengthening dusk, against the trill of insects and the first hootings of the night birds, there began the gathering of a great, oblong pile of brush and logs in the clearing that had been chosen for the night's camp. The animation of the pilgrims gradually increased. Any other night they would have been sullen and exhausted by this time, seeking nothing but their bedrolls. Now they threw themselves enthusiastically into the collection and arrangement of the wood, chuckling and joking, and resorting frequently to one wine skin or another.

The incendiary pile grew high but a central place was left open. There, two of the most gifted of the pilgrims were gradually assembling a wooden framework that took on the rough shape of a human figure as it grew to thrice any human proportions. Then they had to drag one of the carts up into that space so that they could use its bed, and then planks laid across its sides, to continue their work on the upper portions of their creation.

In the half-light of the approaching evening, the figure gradually bestrode the earth like a giant of old. In its hands it wielded a great club, a single branch trimmed to a length of almost a man's trunk. From its back grew wings of woven saplings that spread beyond the figure's width and overtopped its head. The head itself clearly had eyes and a nose, though it lacked any sign of ears and boasted but the merest suggestion of a mouth, and supported a strange, bulbous structure that might suggest a crown or turban. Now, as Simon watched, the whole was beginning to be draped in green forest vine. This trimming hung from the head down over the upper body. Then the cart was drawn carefully away so that everyone could take part in similarly decking the heavy, bulging, lower body of the figure.

The excitement of the participants increased and their approval of the work of their artists was expressed in shouted congratulations to them. The completed whole sat firmly on its base. There was no danger of its tipping over. Under the accumulating weight of vine no parts gave way or sagged enough to distort its terrible outlines. It would be a proper lord of the underworld for this night. Its greenclad body would fill, dominate, bless the center of the grove. It would preside over all of the murmurs, jests, prayers, and vows now commencing in the gathering darkness.

At the four edges of the clearing, fires were being laid and coaxed into lively flame. As they grew, generous numbers of dry branches were collected near them, ready for use. Those of the pilgrim band who had been largely occupied in the gathering of wood back among the trees now ceased their scavanging and came to cluster about one or the other of the outlying fires.

Regretfully, Simon decided that it was time that he should separate himself from what was transpiring. He had seen it often enough in his youth. It was predictable and he knew that he would find it exciting—too exciting—as he always had. Of all the old pagan celebrations, this midsummer's eve was the most vigorous and blatant. He had known priests in his old diocese who danced in it of a night along with their parishoners. As they truly said, there was no preventing it anyway. But the urges that it suggested to him made the little priest apprehensive for himself and for what he wished himself to become. No—it was better to get as far out of sight and earshot as he could. As far as he could—for the surrounding countryside would be full of such fires and such mysteries until the morrow's dawn.

Even as he turned away, there came the sound of the bull's horn repeated again and again. Then, into the silence that followed, the beat of the drums began in slow cadence. At each of the fires on the edges of the clearing, the celebrants jostled to press a branch into the heart of the flame, turning it into a suitable brand. At the same time, the tempo of the drumming gradually increased. Now the horn broke again into sound, urgent, the burly player straining to produce a continuous, inhuman shrieking. The occupants of the grove set up a great shout themselves and raced toward the central pile of wood that stood almost to the height of their heads. All along its perimeter, they plied their brands, setting blaze after blaze.

The horn now ceased but the tempo of the drums increased. The spectators suddenly were hushed, waiting while the small fires along that great pile crept and merged finally into one. The roar of the flames mounted and at last reached a pitch where there was but a single, great blaze in the clearing, as the peripheral fires were kicked apart and their contents fed to that central holocaust.

The parades began. Some of the pilgrims had earlier made their plans for pairing and they joined their hands now, walking the circuit of the blaze that made them sweat and threatened to ignite their very clothing as they danced toward, then away from its maw. As they passed the god of greenery, at the gap in the conflagration on each of its longer sides, they bowed and curtsied to it, some throwing small objects at its foot.

The pilgrim band was largely male and so, thus far, only a fortunate few had been able to find feminine partners in its ranks. But as the fires grew, and at the first sounding of the horn, other women from the surrounding little villages of this country one by one emerged at the edges of the clearing. Animated bargaining and flirtation began almost at once on their appearance. Soon they too had been incorporated into the swirling, dancing throng that circulated more and more rapidly about the great fire. The drums now were a continous roar, competing with that of the flames in an assault on the ears. The dancers had themselves set up a crooning, undulating melody without words. Or perhaps the meaning of the words, long since proscribed, had just been lost.

For some moments now the searing heat of the blaze had been reducing the vegetative garlands of the giant to browning, twisting tendrils. This was joined with the heavy smoke that poured upward from their boiling juices, and from time to time, hid the idol from view completely. But always that looming figure emerged until finally its framework ignited. It was no longer protected by its cloak of greenstuffs.

The fire raced up and along its very frame in a veritable explosion of light. For a brief time, the giant hung there, aflame in every limb, twisting in the heat of its own consummation. Then the few juices left in its entrails sprang into vapor and the violence of their exit threw angry pieces of the dying god in one direction and another. Suddenly, the entire being collapsed in a great shower of sparks and embers. At that, the drums ceased and the whole body of worshippers became silent.

Now the pairs drew apart. One after the other they separated, women going to one side of the fiery clearing where the giant Baal had just subsided into glowing coals. The men drew off to assemble on the opposite side of that gap.

The participants in both groups jostled for the best places and traded excited comments—half insult, half sexual suggestion. But on the side where the men had gathered, skins and buckets of water began to be emptied over some of their number, accompanied by shouts and laughter.

Then one of the youngest, dripping water, leapt through the gap between the piles of glowing embers, over the scattered remains of the midsummer god, and embraced his partner on the far side. For a moment he stamped some random sparks off his feet, before sweeping her up and racing toward the forest. While the company still hooted after those two, another of the men braved the fiery passage to claim his partner. Now they came, one after the other, in quick succession and some unfortunates nursed a raw and burned foot where they had stepped too carelessly. Some were caught in their passage by an explosion of sparks and had to have their persons brushed and slapped free of the glowing debris. But as the ordeal continued, the cooling of the fires and the splashing of water on their clothing made the dash easier for each one who followed.

Martin watched as the clearing emptied and the fire slowly subsided. Now he stood, perhaps a little uncertainly, and wet his feet in the puddles on its verge. Then he picked his way carefully through the gap between the two great berms of glowing coals whose heat radiated in quantities that made him hasten more quickly than he had intended. He was not sure what he himself would do now. He was less sure how Ermentrude would respond. But she was there, on the verge of the forest, alone.

"We have not danced, Ermentrude, but still perhaps you would keep me safe this night?"

The Fleming looked at him long. Head bent, she surveyed him. She spoke in a husky whisper finally.

"You would have me, Martin?"

"I have asked."

"But do you ask for the night only? Or will you take me to your bed for good and all—will you acknowledge me as your woman before all of these pilgrims? We are not children, neither of us, to couple in heat and then to run off heedlessly to play at another game, Martin."

He had not, in fact, been sure of what his offer meant. He knew that the midsummer night had moved him to say more than he had wanted. But the woman had seized her advantage. She was wagering her whole person on this moment. He would play the great fool to try to creep away now, after casting himself in the role of the midsummer swain. The simplicity of her intent moved him strangely. He could not hesitate longer.

"I will have you for my wife, Ermentrude, for this very night and for the days and nights that follow."

A long shudder racked her. It moved in waves as she rose from the log on which she had been seated. The hands that she extended to him now trembled with its passage. As he drew her to him, he came to feel its commotion diffused through her entire body. Then she was sobbing helplessly and it seemed to Martin that her unutterable sadness flowed, at his touch, all through his own being.

Chapter Eight

"**A**nd there were two more, a man from Poitiers and a woman from the Touraine, who died. The usual sort of thing—in their sleep. There was no sign of foul play. Likely it was just the heat, too little food, and exhaustion. We made the usual distribution of their goods and buried them."

Since he had been made the trail boss for the pilgrim band, each evening Martin made some such report of the day's events to the knight. Sometimes there were directions forthcoming for the next day's journey. At other times the knight simply sent him away, having only half listened to what he had to say. But since Rainald had been absent from the camp for three days, celebrating midsummer at the country home of a local magnate of French ancestry, there had been more than usual to relate. The knight had not only listened but had been openly amused throughout. Clearly, the overseer of the pilgrim band was not to be quickly dismissed this evening.

"Sit down, Martin. We have matters to review, you and I, this night. One of my men-at-arms has told me that you have been grossly abusing your little authority in my short absence."

So it is to be the cat and mouse game once again, Martin thought. You have found one sort of amusement with your fellows in the last few days and now you are ready for a little sport at my expense. But he sat, without looking directly at the man. He also did not bother to reply, for the rules of the game were, by now, more than familiar to him. It was not yet his place to speak. The other always had to set the pace.

"Good God, Martin, have you gone sullen on me? You don't speak, even to ask me what are the complaints against you. It may be that you have become too sure of my devotion to justice in these matters.

"In any event, I am told that you have forced the woman Ermentrude into your bed. After all your fine protestations of disinterest and purity of intent, you have yielded to temptation like any ordinary fellow, and violated the woman's virginity most coarsely. She was a virgin, I take it? She always claimed to be—though that is common enough among the sex."

"Her claim was well-founded, my lord. But there was no force involved. We exchanged vows and have become man and wife properly enough."

The knight's smile broadened.

"Properly? Properly? As I have it, you seduced the poor creature on midsummer's eve. One of you was mad with passion, but I doubt that it was that dried up old cow. You, on the other hand, have had two wives already and possess more than enough skill in these matters to lead the spinster astray in the night's heat. She has made no complaint of you, I have heard, but goes shamelessly to your bed each night. The woman is slave to your prowess in passion. You must have made a deep impression on her. I trust that you find at least some poor pleasure in loins so ancient."

It would not do to become angry. That was not his role in this little farce, Martin knew. He was to continue to be the stupid one—at least apparently—and always to seem to misunderstand Rainald's real intent. He was, in that fashion, allowed to defend himself so long as he did it clumsily.

"We did freely cleave to one another on midsummer's eve, truly enough, my lord. Many a marriage has begun so and no one the worse for it. But it is a marriage, not just a random coupling. The priest, Simon, blessed our state after we both expressed our intent and desire."

"Marriage? Without a dowry? Or did she have a fortune in gold tucked up beneath her dirty skirt? Maybe you are the one who was wronged here, Martin. Did she use a magic potion, procured from some other witch?

"Am I to believe that you, whom I have entrusted with the welfare of this whole company when I am away, are so simple a creature that you have been tricked into a marriage that cannot plead even lust to recommend itself. The woman is ugly! Nor do you even have the excuse of greed. Ermentrude scarcely has enough silver to keep her in bread. But for this poor match, this laughable mating, you have once more dared to offend me. I remind you that you owe me your life, Martin."

"She is a good woman, my lord. You have seen that much. And you yourself entrusted her to my care. I considered that you would be pleased, rather than offended, by my action."

Rainald regarded him with mock sobriety for a moment. Then he smiled again and extended the wineskin to him.

"Have some of this. These long interrogations are dry business. But you are getting better at taking my meaning, Martin. Now and then you seem able to follow, even to anticipate, my thoughts. That is very good for one born a farmer. In other circumstances, I could think of making you my steward.

"See how fortunate you are to have someone who appreciates you. A less generous mind than mine might read defiance, or conspiracy, into your actions. Don't you see it? You not only take the woman to bed without my permission but then you have dared to resort to that pious fraud, Simon, to bless your act. You know that I abhor that fat villain and yet you consort with him and even plot with him to excuse your lechery."

"There was no plot, my lord. It was just that Simon is the servant of the Lord God and has the powers to make our wedlock acceptable to Him. It pleased Ermentrude. There was nothing more to it."

"Servant of the Lord! Servant of the Lord? Are we not all servants of the Lord, Martin? In our own fashion do we not all serve His will?

"Suppose I put it to you, Martin, that you are corrupt. There is a neat little bargain struck here between the three of you. The woman makes you a gift of her body—such as it is. God alone knows why you should want such a drab, but apparently you are a slave to your baser passions. Ermentrude, for her part, understands well enough that your position as day-to-day leader of this pilgrim band gives you certain opportunities. Women are quick to such connivance.

"Now then, both you and your paramour—too grand a term for your partner, Martin?—realize that there will be muttering and complaint among the pilgrims when you bestow your mutual favors on one another. So you have recourse to this priest. He makes your carnal traffic licit, even holy, but at a price.

"Then you use your work-a-day authority to modify my express arrangements. Simon no longer has to drive one of the carts like the cowardly churl that he is. Instead he sits in one and spends his time surveying the countryside—like a gentleman. The cart, instead, is driven by Ermentrude. She is at least clever enough to manage oxen and now she rides rather than walks. For a little nightly play, the Fleming has elevated her status, we might say.

"Do you see how it all fits, my friend? You employ the small place I have given you to bend others to your will and then reward them for their submission just as though you had some right to it. What is an honest lord to make of all this?"

As always, the knight's jests and wordplay held a latent menace that might flare into sudden violence if the response of the tormented was inappropriate in his eyes. Feigned stupidity was a refuge. Even if its artificiality were clear to both of them, it represented the sort of compliance that Rainald exacted as his continuing due.

Martin spread his hands, sidewards, palms up.

"We are simpler people than that, my lord. Simon tore the flesh of his leg on a tripod pole. For the present he finds it difficult to walk or even to stand in a jolting cart. So now he sits on a cookpot while Ermentrude drives. Even the dullest pilgrim can hardly see much exaltation in that.

"Ermentrude drives because the walking was killing her. She was no longer strong enough continually to bear even her own weight. The swelling of her joints was making her dizzy with pain before half the day was out. Before long she would have become another corpse just like the two we buried the other day. I have made these arrangements because they both needed help and because they could help one another. This way your pilgrimage goes on with less delay."

Wordlessly, Rainald again extended him the wineskin. Then the interrogator leaned back, and clasped one knee between his hands. The habitual mockery in his voice was replaced by a certain softness and his entire manner seemed gentler in the firelight.

"You almost convince me of your simplicity, my friend. But what of the woman? What business is she of yours? She is going to die in any event—and soon enough if I am any judge of such things. On your own admission, you've buried two wives already. Yet you persist in turning pleasure into penance."

"May I remind my lord that the need of penance is why I

make this journey? But there is more to it than that. The woman needs help. She needs some little hope. I wonder myself if she is not already too weakened by this pilgrimage to last much longer. But she needed some comfort and it somehow seemed little enough to offer her a share of my bed."

The other chuckled briefly, but not unkindly.

"I doubt much that she would thank you for such sentiment. I have found her a proud bitch who puts her own worth high for the miserable vessel that she bears it in. Man, she wants you to pant after her or, at the very least, to pretend to desire her in the face of others. She would screech like the very fiends of hell to hear you speak of comforting her when she likely needs beyond all else in her own mind to be able to regard herself as comfort to you."

"I think that is very probably true. But there is hardly more that I can do for her. We should both appear foolish indeed in the role of young lovers."

"And so you and your 'comfort' are a reproach to her. Do you see, Martin, that this measured virtue of yours is an offense to others as well as to me. You are not a stripling any longer, true, but your manhood is still green enough to grace some lusty foolishness and more than a little vice. Indulge it! Sin some! You'll be forgiven for it by the world a lot quicker than for this unctuous, gloomy rectitude of yours."

Martin pondered his response for a bit. This was new ground. Was Rainald really offering him such license? Could he escape the other's cold enmity—perhaps even come out of this journey with his life? What might feigned compliance buy him?

"I suppose that I have as much experience of avarice and other sins as most men, my lord. But I have not found much in the way of pleasure in them. What I did find is the grief that bought me here. I had hopes, I still have hopes, that this pilgrimage to Saint James will purge me somehow and that I will find peace, a little contentment, and forgiveness finally."

"Pleasure? Peace? You disappoint me, Martin. I had begun to think that you were a man. No wonder you can't enjoy your little episodes of sin. You must keep looking back to some childish dream of happiness. Do you really still believe that this world of ours has anything to do with peace? When we bury your precious Ermentrude, will you be the happier for it? You can't save her—or Simon either. You can't even save yourself. Just like all of those two-legged cattle that troop along after us, day by day, we have no destination but the butcher finally. Your precious Saint James won't change that. He's a true servant of God, he is. His role is to get us to bend our neck's to the ax. He did that with his own. That's why he is a saint."

The ordinary, studied lassitude of the knight had dropped away. He was intent now. His eyes flashed and his words came hard, fast, exact.

"There is some steel in you, Martin. Use it! Let it out! So you haven't found happiness in your little escapades, whatever they might have been. You choose the wrong sins, man. You pick the soft ones, the common ones. You spoke of avarice. How common! A tradesman's sin. You spoke of lust. Any ninny can indulge that. Murder is what you need. The sensation that comes with seeing someone grovel—someone who knows that they are going to die at your hand. There's some real excitement in that.

"I think that you might be up to a really serious vice, my friend. That is why I have bothered with you at all. Suppose, just suppose, that when you go to your bed tonight you start by caressing that old bitch, Ermentrude. You get her all worked up, slavering with delight in her vision of her own desirability. Then, when you are on top of her, you put your hands about her throat and choke, ever so slowly you choke, so that she has time to know that she is going to die. She has time to know that you have betrayed her into hell. Don't you think that you might be able to do that, Martin? Can't you imagine how exciting it might be?"

"I suspect that if I did, my lord, you would have me hanged the next morning."

Rainald laughed delightedly at this rejoinder.

"So I might, Martin, so I might! On the other hand, I might instead promote you to be my steward. What does that matter? Will you have the soul of a peasant forever? Will you forever burden yourself with these mean little calculations of what will come next? Whatever happened next, you would have been a man—for the moment at least. You would have lived! For once, for a moment, you would have been master of your own life."

There was no soft way out of this trap into which he had been maneuvered, Martin reflected. In any event, he was tired—too tired and repelled to be properly cautious. But he must be judicious about just how he framed his reply. He spoke hesitantly, quietly. "Suppose then, my lord, I dare to tell you that what you propose is madness. It is nothing less. What if I should grant, for a moment, that what you have always accused me of doing, opposing your will, is what indeed I have been doing. I have befriended Simon, in part, exactly because you persecute him. I spoke for the Flemish woman, in part, because it would have given you pleasure that morning to see her die. Am I not master of my own life, for a moment and perhaps no more now, precisely because I have chosen to thwart your will in these things? Do I not knowingly risk the consequences. I have seen you kill."

To his surprise the knight again smiled—genuinely, broadly. Once more Martin was offered the wineskin and once more he took it. His hands shook a little with the intensity of his feelings. He also realized with some alarm that he was becoming more than a little drunk.

"You prove once again that you are an honest man, Martin. It gives me hope for you. That is the sole reason that you find yourself here now, alive and drinking wine with me. If you were not so honest, I should have finished with you long since. And so, you too are a little mad, my friend. You risk your own life for a cleric who is a coward always and a hypocrite as often as he needs be. You risk your life for a wornout, despairing old sow who is on the verge of dropping dead in her tracks anyway. Yet you do say that I propose madness?

"The world is mad, Martin. Here we are, the whole company of us, walking half way to the end of the earth. For what? When we reach Santiago de Compostela, if we do, what shall we have accomplished? Will our sins be washed away? We will be quick enough to commit new ones, won't we? Will we be cured of gout, rheumatism, the pox? Won't we be visited with new afflictions soon enough to replace them?

"But we walk. Well, you common folk walk anyway, and strain your guts, and accumulate your blisters, and cadge swill for food from one another and from the farmers we pass along the way, which sours your stomachs and gives you the trots at night. But this very night, some bandit may steal into the camp and crush your head with a rock while you sleep your more or less innocent sleep. Or tomorrow Julius may finally succeed in biting you—he dreams of it, you know—and in a day or two you could sicken, swell, and die. Or one of your fellow pilgrims may find a way to poison you for his portion in the sharing out of your miserable goods.

"Who then is sane, Martin? Those who drag themselves from day to miserable day afraid to live—whose most noble hope is to put off dying for yet another moon? No matter the pretense, even the dullest of them knows that they are dying. No one can elude that certainty for more than a moment or two at a time. Are these sane beings, Martin, who crawl about the world in such fashion?

"If you can steel yourself to be so honest with me, why not be honest with yourself? Be so brave as to dare to steal some little share of God's power for yourself. Don't you think that He tires of all these puling, whining cowards? Might He not admire some one of His creatures with courage enough to wield His own rough justice in this morass, this sinkhole, to which He has committed us? Afterall, imitation is the real flattery, is it not? Perhaps it might be the sincerest form of worship as well."

Rainald stopped suddenly and peered closely at him. It occurred to Martin that the knight too might just have discovered that he himself was becoming inebriated. The latter's dignity would not allow such an association and he pulled himself up with just visible effort.

"I see that I have strayed into matters that are new to you, my friend. Think on them. Think on them as you go off to your Flemish lover. I will be curious to see if she still lives in the morning. Think on what an interesting journey this oh-too-ordinary pilgrimage could be—for the two of us."

He rose, turned away, and Martin knew that he had survived the interview once more. When he found his way back to his bedroll, Ermentrude was there, awake, waiting on his return. She was relieved but angry.

"So once more he has let you come away alive. The man is a devil. You are a fool to bandy words with him, Martin. No good can come of it. What did he say about us?"

Martin drew her to him and folded her in his arms. She made no resistance but began to shudder violently. Is it passion or grief, he wondered? She was such a raw person. She was so accustomed to the stiffness of her own body that it seemed to hurt her to relax into compliance with its natural desires.

Strange, he thought, that she should be so tall. She fits my needs so more evenly than did Claire or Therese.

"I do not think that he much loves us, Ermentrude."

To giggle was perhaps beyond her. It was too late in her life for the simplicities of levity. Instead, she butted her head against his jaw in gentle but fond reproach for his refusal to be serious.

"You are such a good fool, Martin. It will be your death. But I love you for it."

Chapter Nine

The pale blue of the morning sky was beginning to turn a grey-white that forced one to squint in order to see clearly for any distance. The western breeze steadily became less of a solace and more of a chafing irritant—the fine dust that it bore assaulting the eyelids. By the time that the sun reached zenith its weight would be inhuman. If the pilgrims could find some adequate grove of pin oaks by then, they would rest in its shade until the afternoon breeze offered some prospect of enduring the further march that would bring them to a camp site shortly before twilight.

This routine was now predictable. They had repeated it so often, and suffered its oppression so regularly, that its burden and their endurance of it was largely mechanical. Unless someone in the column fell, and died where he fell, the apathy of the pilgrims ordinarily went unbroken.

But this morning had proved unusual from its very start. Orders from the knight had come to his men-at-arms before they had eaten breakfast that they should wear their mail shirts over their tunics. Their grumbling had started immediately. The prospect of the morning march, clad in metal that would swiftly become a little furnace under the summer sun, made a bad beginning to a day whose signs from the very sunrise promised suffocating heat. The pilgrims avoided them as much as they could. Rainald's men were a brutal, ugly-tempered lot and the unexpected command made them even worse.

Rainald himself appeared in his chainmail tunic and his helmet, glittering, hung from his saddle. Its long, horsehair plume fluttered golden as Alexander stamped and swung his massive bulk uneasily from side to side. The stallion, too, sensed trouble in the break in the regular rhythms of the journey. He was not accustomed to being saddled so early, if at all, for his master rode the palfrey as a matter of course most days. Still less did Alexander expect to find a helmet bumping about his shoulder and his master in the additional weight of chainmail on his back.

Rainald appeared completely at ease, resplendent in an overtunic of silver and scarlet threads worked into a forest-green background. His longsword swung easily from the belt about his waist. The shaft of a short, throwing javelin jutted from its leather case at his right knee, well clear of the hilt of the sword. The knight's long lance sat with its heel secured in a leather cup by his right foot. His right hand supported its middle length negligently and effortlessly, seemingly oblivious to the burden of its gleaming steel tip and the family pennons that fluttered in the breeze of morning just below that shining threat. Surely he was conscious of the appearance that he made, as splendid as it was unusual, but he gave no sign that he recognized the surprise of the pilgrim band or the curiosity that it aroused.

For his part, Martin had been sweating since daybreak. When the knight had ordered him to saddle Alexander, the trouble had begun. The big stallion had been restive from the first but even more troublesome had been the reaction of Julius. Almost at once the smaller stallion's eyes had taken on a dangerous glint when he realized that he was to have the entire day in the proximity of the mare. The palfrey excited him. But, like his master, Rainald, Julius could disguise the extent of his plotting. The knight had made no explanation for the changes to Martin. Only orders had been given. Beyond them, Rainald had questioned his ostler and trail boss in the most ordinary fashion.

"Ermentrude is well this morning, I trust? I have seen her about already this day and she seems no worse for the night."

Without waiting a reply, he had taken the reins of Alexander and moved off. With that, Julius's testing of Martin had begun. Steadily he drifted in the direction of the lovely palfrey, straining ever so lightly against the lead rope in Martin's hands. When he was checked, the stallion yielded, only to resume his sidling toward his would-be love the moment that the ostler relaxed that tension even slightly.

Martin had entrusted the lead rope for the mare to one of the brighter pilgrims, a man called Amos. This man was mature and had some experience with animals and the mare was gentle enough in most circumstances. But the advances of Julius were making that quiet beast more restive. She had kicked, tentatively, a number of times as the morning wore on and the pilgrim was becoming less certain of how to control her. Martin had reacted by increasing the distance between Julius and the palfrey but the stallion strove against his efforts and that fool, Amos, sought to allay his own uncertainty by bringing himself and the female closer to Martin and his unruly charge.

Now things were made worse as the column creaked and jolted to a halt. At its head, Rainald waved for Martin to come up and the trail boss rounded on his harassed assistant.

"Get the mare back there behind the last cart and tie her up to it. Then stay there and try to gentle her down. Feed her just a little and stroke her lightly. Now, man, do it now!"

When Amos moved off, Martin turned his full attention to Julius. The stallion pulled toward the female but Martin worked the bit at the end of his lead rope savagely in the horse's mouth. For a moment he thought that the brute was about to rear and strike at him. Then the horse thought better of it. He could wait on a contest that he was surely, if slowly, winning. The stallion permitted Martin to move him toward the knight although he hung back just enough to put a strain on his lead. He had no intention of giving over in the struggle.

"Careful with that horse's mouth, Martin! Steeds of good blood are like women, you know. If you would get the best performance from them, you have to go about it gently."

The man was at his sardonic best. Then his eyes flicked away briefly.

"Take our dear Julius over to the left side of the first cart and make him fast. You can take care that he is fully secured for we are going to tarry here for just a bit. Hobble him if need be. Then come back to me. Don't be too long at it."

When Martin returned, the knight was looking off toward a small stream some distance to the west. There was a tiny copse on the near bank, to the north of the cartpath. Just before that grove of trees a band of mounted men were milling about confusedly. From what he could see they numbered about a dozen.

"Look at those oafs, Martin. Simply by stopping we have thrown them into complete confusion. Their plans have now to be remade and they are not certain what to do."

He looked at his trail boss questioningly. When Martin remained silent, he smiled. There was a certain excitement about him now.

"Our compatriot, my host of a few days back, told me over dinner that we might encounter some trouble when we reached this stream. He said that it had been reported that a group of brigands had set up a toll station of their own at this ford and were extorting payment for its passage from pilgrim bands that wished to cross. Did you note that they have been tracking us since morning?"

"I have been busy with your animals, my lord. I had no leisure to look about."

"I saw that, Martin. But I have a different task for you now. You see, those louts expected that we would approach right up to the banks of that rivulet and take some rest in the shade of those trees. A reasonable enough expectation, given the time of day, the heat, and the need for water. But when we stopped short here, they were thown into confusion. A good sign, Martin, a good sign. Slow thinkers, that bunch. But they will be along presently, you may count on it. We should make some preparations, don't you think?"

"There would seem to be more than a dozen of them, my lord. They will outnumber you and your men-at-arms by two to one or even more."

"Just so, Martin. That is why we need to prepare. One mustn't be careless about this sort of thing."

The noble was obviously enjoying the situation. His casual demeanor remained but Martin could see the small vein in his throat beating more rapidly and his nostrils had a slight flare as his breath came more quickly.

"They won't be able to see what we are doing from where they are now. I want you and Albert around to the other side of the carts. Albert can get in the third one and you should take the last. Each of you should take up station as if you meant to drive. Reins in hand, you know. But both of you will have your bows with you on the floor of the cart. I don't want those bandits to see your bows unless it is necessary to use them.

"The rest of my men will attend me where I am now. Pass the word to the pilgrims to remain together and behind the last cart. I don't want them in the way. If there is a fight, I will yell to you whom you are to kill. But only the first one. After that I shall be busy and you and Albert will have to use your own judgment as to what is best.

"Can you kill someone, Martin? Albert is pretty good at it if he has proper leadership."

He looked sharply at his trail boss. Martin could feel his own heart starting to pump more swiftly.

"I have never yet killed a man, my lord."

"Well, don't make a fuss about it, Martin. It is sometimes surprisingly easy to do. Especially once you realize that your own life is at risk. But then, perhaps we shall not have to fight at all this morning."

But looking at the man, seeing his excitement, Martin knew that there would indeed be a fight. Rainald would provoke one even if it could be avoided. Alexander, too, understood that. The big stallion could feel the tension in the thighs of his master and knew from experience what that meant. Without further instruction, Martin moved to the far side of the row of carts, followed by Albert. Both men rolled their bows and quivers over the side and into the bed, then swung themselves into the driver's position and took up the reins and whip.

The band by the wood took Martin and Albert's action as a sign that the pilgrims were about to move off and decided then to approach.

As they strung out in a rough line their numbers, twenty in all, became evident. All were mounted in some fashion but they were a sorry-looking lot, Martin thought. A third of them were on donkeys. The horses of the rest were skinny nags, a couple of them almost lame it seemed, and stunted as was so common in this country.

As they closed now, the men could be seen largely to match their mounts. They wore the rough woolens of countryfolk, ragged and patched, and their sandaled feet were stuffed into leather stirrups. Only four or five of them had boots. Their arms were of the same sort. While a few had spears, and all had swords, none but the man who rode in front, the leader obviously, had a helmet or chainmail. For protection they relied on shields, some the kite-shaped sort of the mounted man but many of them the round targes of the foot soldier.

Rainald had advanced a few lengths from the first cart, accompanied by one of his men-at-arms to whom he now handed his heavy, pennoned lance to plant in the roadway. The knight had donned his helmet and its horsehair plume swayed ever so slightly in the hot breeze. The other three of his men remained by the first of the carts, shields and spears at the ready.

The strangers hardly knew what to make of this gorgeous peacock who sat silently and with empty hands, awaiting their approach. A horse's length from him they drew up. The latter part of their column drifted to the right, flanking the pilgrim band in the roughest of fashions. But a half-dozen of the best-mounted were bunched close to the leader, facing Rainald.

"We bid you welcome, sir knight, to León and the kingdom of the great Alfonso, son of the great Fernando."

Their spokesman was a middle-aged man, bronzed and lean. His mail was mostly intact, if worn and dull and his helmet had seen much service as well. His dark eyes surveyed the group of pilgrims in frank assessment. From what he could see of them they seemed an ordinary enough lot. Some pickings but not the sort that would make you rich. Then there was this youth with the great stallion and rings enough on his fingers to feed his own men for a year. There were the horses too, of course. They had come over the mountains, sure enough. Not much of that kind of horseflesh here, or even in the south among the Africans. The young gentleman, clearly he was that, just sat there, smiling faintly. He had made no reply.

"You must understand, sir, that this pathway is a toll road

and King Alfonso requires us to collect it of all passersby just at the river up there. We hope that you and your people will not find that inconvenient. Surely it cannot be unexpected."

"What does surprise me," the answer came silkily and hardly loud enough to hear, "is that your King Alfonso is such a barebones, ragtag king as to employ stable sweepings like yourselves to conduct his business."

The other stiffened in anger. This young bastard just sat there, making no move, smiling at him. For some reason, he wasn't taking them seriously. It was peculiar. Still, he only had a few soldiers with him, for all that his armor was rich and finely made. Better get it done then.

"Soldiers such as ourselves are seldom pretty, my lord. Still, a stranger in the land like yourself has no call to insult our king. We have our duty to perform and you and your companions can make good the toll with horses, or jewelry if you lack coin."

His eyes turned for a moment to signal his immediate companions. Back where the pilgrims had huddled together, fearing the outcome, some of the brigands had approached quite closely. One of them had already dismounted from his mule and was now pulling one of the women from among the pilgrims.

"Martin, kill me that man."

Rainald's voice carried clear and steady in the hush. Martin stooped and gathered up his war bow, already strung. The shaft, leaving the bow, flew true. He knew it as soon as he felt the release. The arrow's head struck the man in the side below his armpit and the shock of the impact rocked him on his feet. His hat slipped off his head and he swayed. The woman he had gripped now began to scream and pummel him about the face and head. Then he fell backward and the woman, overbalanced herself, fell on top of him, still screaming and punching at his face until the blood began to erupt from his mouth.

Before the man had struck the ground, Rainald had drawn his sword in a sudden sweeping motion that totally belied his seeming indolence of a moment before. He spurred Alexander forward and the great stallion surged violently at the touch of the steel. Before the bandit chief could react, the space to his immediate right was cleared as the knight struck with the point of his sword into the unprotected belly of his companion. The man's round shield gave him no protection. As he crumpled forward in the saddle, trying to keep his life from pouring out of the gaping hole in his abdomen, his mount sensed the sudden lack of control by the thing on his back and shied violently to the left.

Rainald's knees now directed Alexander and the great stallion understood the message exactly. He threw his bulk against the shoulders of the bandit chieftain's mount, pressing against the slighter horse. It scrabbled sideways, feeling for footing on the stony surface while its master sought an unprotected target for his sword. But the knight was too close to allow him a full stroke anywhere and Rainald's shield anticipated his every thrust. The other brigands bunched behind their chieftain maneuvered to clear the mortally wounded man's horse, and to find room to come at the knight unhindered by one another. Being without defensive armor, they took good care. Their enemy's sword seemed to be everywhere, anticipating and deflecting their spear thrusts.

In a moment it was over. The smaller horse lost its footing and went over on its side in the dust, trapping the leg of its rider underneath. Alexander wheeled and broke free of the press in that same moment. There was just enough time, while his remaining enemies hesitated before this unexpected turn, for Rainald to gain a few lengths, to let his sword drop free to the extent of its tether, and to pull the throwing spear from its casing. Standing in the stirrups, while the stallion froze in response, he hurled the javelin true. As it crashed through the chest of his nearest adversary, the knight had already retrieved his sword and had put the big horse into renewed charge against the remaining four of the group.

To a man, they broke. Wheeling in all directions, they fled before this madman. The latter did not pursue them. His own men-at-arms were hard pressed.

After Martin's initial shot, the nearest companion of the downed man had urged his donkey into a furious charge. Shouting as he came, he evidently expected the bowman to panic. Within ten feet of Martin, the man realized that he had not wavered. At that distance, his eyes betrayed his tardy intention to pull up and draw off, but it was too late for that. At pointblank range, the shaft was loosed and the bandit crashed to the ground while his donkey skidded to a halt just short of the cart.

With a moment to breath freely, Martin turned toward the head of the column of carts. In the second cart from him, Albert was dying. He too had gotten off an unanticipated shot at the brigands and one of them now sat on his mount a little way off, frantically attempting to work an arrow out of his right side. But two of his friends had immediately charged Albert's cart. The bowman managed to get off another shot which caught one of their donkeys full in its chest. The startled beast stopped abruptly but its rider swung off and loped the remaining distance to the cart. He and his still mounted companion were now engaged in stabbing to death the hapless Albert, pinned against the side of his cart.

Martin fired at them, in haste, and the arrow whistled closely past the face of the still-mounted one who swung down and, with his fellow, began to work toward the bowman. They took opposite sides of the carts and stayed close to the protecting wood as they advanced.

At the head of the column, Rainald's four remaining men-at-arms were hard beset by twice that number of assailants. That they wore mail and their opponents did not, partly made up for the fact that they were afoot while the former were mounted. Even so, they were barely able to offer an adequate defense and one of them had already been bloodied.

Now the lead cart, which had served to defend their backs, was beginning to draw off. Simon the priest and Ermentrude were both huddled in its bed and the reins were slack. The ox team that drew it had now been thoroughly alarmed by the din and had begun to plod off in the direction of the stream ahead. Rainald's men were attempting to move crabwise along with the cart, as not to lose its protection. But it was hard to concert this action as the attackers pressed their new advantage.

The slaughter in the making was averted by the knight himself. Freed by the flight of his earlier adversaries, he now charged down behind the bandits, almost decapitating the rearmost of their number with a slashing blow before they were aware of this new threat. Rainald's momentum carried him past the little knot of men, but he pulled up short and wheeled, returning to the attack on their other flank where the crash of Alexander's bulk bowled over a donkey and rider. The surprise he created allowed one of his men to score a lucky spear thrust, tumbling another of their assailants from the saddle.

With the odds suddenly shifted against them, the remaining bandits chose to run for safety. Before they could clear though another of them was ridden down and dispatched from behind by the knight. The two dismounted men stalking Martin farther down the column now became conscious of the desertion of their companions. Running for their single mount, they swung up on it and galloped to the north riding double. Martin chose not to try a shot at them. It was over.

Meanwhile, the leader of the bandits had managed to struggle to his feet, supporting himself on a spearshaft. The fall by his horse had seriously injured his right leg. One of the fleeing bandits halted long enough to haul him up, unceremoniously, by his arm and then by his swordbelt until he lay across the haunches of his mount. He then continued his flight, his chieftain bouncing and clutching at all possible handholds.

For a moment it appeared that Rainald was disposed to pursue his routed adversaries. But after surveying the pilgrim column and his own men briefly, he decided against it. Instead he rode up after the first cart, rumbling on its unattended way toward the river ahead.

"Mistress Ermentrude. If you will scramble up from the cart bed and take the reins of your team again, it will save you both a bath. You might also tell our fearless priest crouching down there, that he can sit up and leave off his prayers for a bit."

To the surprise of most, he then set about reorganizing the column for the remainder of the day's travel as though little or nothing of import had happened. Albert's body was wrapped and loaded in a cart for later burial at the evening's campsite. The wounded man-at-arms was bundled, protesting against the bad luck of it, into the same cart. The enemy dead, or near dead, were simply dragged together about a large boulder that lay to the right of the pathway. All nine of them were simply left there at the knight's insistence and when some of the pilgrims began to approach the human pile, he reacted violently.

"Leave them alone! Get away from them, you carrion jackels! At least they died like men, fighting. That's something none of you will ever do. If their friends come back to bury them, well and good. If not the birds of the air and the wolves will do their last rites. So it is that real heroes perish. They're in good company. Maybe for the first time in their lives. Now, move ahead. Move ahead. We need to put a little distance between ourselves and those corpses. It will be a fair time yet before we have a decent place to hide from the sun this day."

Chapter Ten

"**S**o now you kill for him."

The words came out of a silence that he had found comfortable. The three of them were sitting a short distance from the dying embers of the cooking fire. The evening breeze had begun and the heat of the day was becoming little more than a memory. Over the plain a thin band of cloud caught the waning rays of the sun, turning itself into mountains, and lizards, and aerial rivers as it drifted almost imperceptibly along the horizon's line.

Martin glanced sidelong at Ermentrude. He wanted to discover what had moved her to speak so. He did not wish to betray how much she had startled him. That she should choose to break out so violently beside Simon was a measure of her emotion.

But he had no chance to avoid the directness of her gaze. Her great eyes were full and their waters, it seemed to him, ready to flow over. She bent forward, elbows upon her knees and head cupped in her hands. The woman's skin was tanned to the consistency of old leather and the lines of it were deep and many. Yet he thought again, as he had often of late, that it was drawn ever more tightly over the bones of her cheeks and chin. Even the fact that she now rode in the lead cart, rather than walked, seemed to him to have slowed but not halted her decline.

The summer sun was pitiless. On the plains there was no escaping it throughout the day's travel. At night and during noontime rest some shelter could be found, but otherwise the scorching rays had to be borne. They struck even through one's clothing and weakened the body as they dulled the spirit. The ever-present heat added to the growing debility from the scarceness of food. Everyone in the pilgrim band was beginning to wonder now how long their small hoard of coin would last. The odds and ends of edibles that the farmers along the route brought in to their nightly encampments were increasingly expensive. The pilgrims before them and those to come increased the natives' confidence of their sale.

The pilgrims reacted by eating more sparingly and the practice weakened further their resistance to the erosion the relentless travel worked on their bodies. Martin and Simon pooled their food purchases and fed the common pot that they kept with Ermentrude. Even so, her pride reacted against too obvious attempts to treat her as an invalid, though it was ever more difficult to ignore what she was becoming. The juices of her body seemed every day to be thinner—still the force of her person had a violence about it which spoke to a strength that might be desperate but was far from completely spent.

"You mean those robbers the other day?"

"Don't be stupid with me, husband."

Simon stirred, as if to rise, and then thought better of it. This promised a major quarrel between his two friends and he was loath to be drawn into it. He had no particular hope of resolving it, but running away was too obvious. He would stay and be embarrassed. It was better.

"What else could I have done? We were attacked. Rainald needed my help."

"He commanded your help because he knew that he could get it. You carry his bow. That savage says 'go' and you go; he says 'come' and you come."

"But he is in command of this pilgrimage. He has asked me to help with the work of it and I agreed. I thought we all had agreed. What happened was just a part of my duty."

Martin was uneasy making such an argument in front of Simon. His friend had not forgiven the knight for usurping the leadership of the band. He looked at the little priest and raised his shoulders, half in apology. But the cleric in turn raised his eyebrows. He understood the farmer's need to save himself and tried to signal as much.

"Duty! Oh the world is so full of 'duty,' isn't it? You both know that he provoked that fight, don't you? He's a killer, our leader. There's nothing that man enjoys more than his glorious cutting and slashing and watching someone's blood gush out at his hand. And now you've begun to help him kill and maim."

"But you yourself saw what was about to happen, woman. The man I shot first was pulling that woman out of our band. The second robber attacked me then, and I was but defending myself. What would you have had me do? What do you think was going to happen to the woman—to all of you?"

"Nothing that hasn't happened to her before, I'll bet. And much the same, probably, as will happen to her again. I care nothing for all of your hypocritical defense of virginity and honor."

She almost shouted at him. Once again he knew that they were arguing in front of an audience—an amused audience. He was the typical husband on the defensive, belabored by a furious wife. He strained to keep his own voice low so that it would not carry to the curious among the pilgrims standing about smiling, happy to be entertained by his predicament.

"That is not a fair answer, Ermentrude; it is not even a true one. You yourself killed a man we all knew for just such an attempt on a girl who was not even a member of our party. You would do the same again."

If his argument took her aback, the woman did not immediately show it.

"I did not intend to kill him. That was an accident. He had a thin neck. I just wanted to stop him from abusing that pathetic little creature."

"But, in any event, you did what you thought was your duty. It isn't so easy to judge is it? You couldn't just look away and stop up your ears. What did I do that is so different?"

She looked at him exasperated, as if he were a particularly stupid child. Suddenly she was weeping.

"It does not matter what I did or didn't do. I am dying, you fool. But you will live! And that monster is turning you from a gentle, good-hearted farmer into one of his rotten murderers. You still have a life, Martin. For God's sake, keep it your own. For my sake."

With surprising quickness, she was up and running blindly. No one interfered with her going. Martin decided against following her into the growing dusk.

In a little bit, he spoke to the priest. Embarrassed Simon had continued to sit, avoiding his eyes.

"Do you understand her? You are a man of peace, a man of God. Is she right? You didn't get involved in the fight. Should I have stayed out of it too? Let anything at all happen and just stay the hell out of it?"

He was conscious of a sort of aggrieved belligerence in his own voice. He was ashamed of it but he wanted to win the argument with his friend that he could not win with that woman.

"My actions are not the point, my friend. I cannot fight. I'm afraid that, if I strike at someone, they will strike me back and I will be hurt—or at least made to look foolish. So my actions are not a model for anyone."

Simon paused for a moment. Then he continued in the same apologetic tone.

"In any event, she may not even really care what you did. What she hates to think is that you risked your own life for Rainald. She's jealous, I think. You know how we ride, day by day, in the cart. Since my leg has improved, we take turns with the reins. But all the time she talks. Dear God, how she talks!"

He shook his little, round head at the memory.

"So I know that the greatest event in her entire life, as she sees it, was that you risked your life to save her's. Your interference to save her that day was a miracle in her eyes. No one she ever knew had cared so much. Till then Ermentrude had always been a lone woman, plain and propertyless. If people had considered her at all, it was with a scarcely concealed contempt. So I doubt that even your subsequent taking her into your bed, though it meant very much to her pride, had the same character for her. You saved a life that she herself had ceased to care about.

"So she is jealous of your devotion. She is furious that you should risk yourself for the sake of the knight. That you accept his orders.

"She knows that she is dying, you know. She knows that she cannot have you much longer. Above all, she does not want Rainald to enjoy your service. In a strange sort of fashion, the knight is her rival and a threat to the dignity that your attentions have bestowed on her."

Martin gazed at his cleric friend with new respect. Simon had understood more about the woman than he himself had.

"But what do I do then? I can't just leave in the middle of

the night—with or without Ermentrude. If I took her, Rainald would hunt us down simply enough. If I left her, he would find a pretext to kill her just out of revenge and wounded pride.

"Can I do anything but continue to do exactly what I have done so far? I accepted his offer to serve as trail boss so I could protect her a little better. It meant that I could let her ride and spare her some of this eternal walking that is draining her strength so quickly. But our local devil probably understood what you have just said. He somehow knew that it would set her—and even you yourself in some measure—against me. He envies us our friendship, I think."

The priest smiled and shifted his bulk. The night was coming on rapidly and they had lost their audience. It was easier for confidences now.

"You have not lost my trust, Martin. You are a good man and I understand how little freedom you have to do anything but what Rainald chooses. I realize that you are protecting me as well as Ermentrude by what you do. I understand that you have no choice but to continue as you have been and to hope that, in some fashion, it will all work out.

"At the same time, we all know that you are not going to be able to keep Ermentrude alive. She realizes that, too. At the same time, she is happy that you are giving her a bit more time to spend as your wife and furious that you do it by bending to the will of a man she hates. She is not a stupid woman, your wife. And she is frightened, of course. We are all afraid when we get that close to death.

"So you must try to ease her fears and her anger. Do what you must but don't appear enthusiastic. Don't look as though you enjoy your position for a moment. You can't do better than that for now. At least, I can't see how you might."

Martin considered his friend's words with a wry grimace.

He was not sure that he had expected a solution from Simon. But the advice he had received mirrored so precisely what he himself had already concluded that it was close to no help at all. He could not avoid some impatience creeping into his voice.

"How is it that I decide on a pilgrimage to atone for the death of two wives and find myself faced with the likelihood of burying yet another? I didn't want this woman, God knows. She's no beauty. I became her protector simply to save her life. I took her to wife only because she was so forlorn. Now I find myself bending to her will far more completely than I would, or will, to Rainald—for all his threats."

Simon was glad that it was now full dusk. The priest knew that his friend needed the privacy that the dark afforded such naked feelings. In turn, that gave Simon the opportunity to speak freely without intruding too directly.

"Perhaps, Martin, you are being brought finally to understand what it was that you undertook when you assented to making this pilgrimage as an act of penitence. Did you hope that when you had reached Compostela, out there at the end of the world, that you would find peace? Was it, in your mind, to be a gift of the saint so long as you finally in some way reached his shrine? That would have been a true miracle, wouldn't it? It is the kind of miracle that little children and the very simple of mind dream about.

"But then, you would have skipped the pilgrimage, would you not? It is the journey, quite as much as the destination, that changes us, don't you think? You have said more than once that it was not your choice to fall in with us back there outside of Jaca. True enough. Rainald recruited you none too gently. But perhaps that was the real beginning of your penance. Monks, you know, locate the true origin of a reformed life in the very act of the acceptance of obedience to the will of another."

Even in the dark, Simon could sense that his friend had started—was about to speak.

"No. Don't interrupt me just yet. Think for a moment about what you told me long since. The guilt that you owned then, the matter for which you thought that you must do some kind of penance, was what? That you loved your two former wives too well, too violently? That their beauty and your lust carried you into the neglect of everything else, even their wellbeing?

"Is it simply ironic, then, that now you find yourself subject to the will of a woman whom you refuse to bring yourself to say that you love? You say that she is plain and so she is. She is old, even to the point of death itself, and yet she holds you fast. People in our little band laugh at you for the way that she commands your service and, so far at least, you submit to that. To an enemy, the punishment would seem to have been cunningly contrived to fit the sin."

After a bit, Martin's voice came out of the darkness. Simon could detect the strain in it.

"You know, my friend, that I value your help and your advice. What you say has much point to it. Ermentrude may well be the medicine I need—in some sense anyway. But you have not buried two wives. You do not know the pain of that. If I could preserve Ermentrude's life, save her, such a penance would have more to recommend it. I don't think that your God, or you yourself, ought to require her to die so that I may be forgiven. It would be more just if I were to be the one to die instead."

"Maybe, Martin, this is not the time to speak about justice. It is important, very important, that you have come to speak about your wife with the voice of love. You just have, you know. But all that we can do for the present, I think, is to endure.

"Each day, when I see Rainald's face, I think once more of my friend, Gerald. Then I wish the knight dead. That he walks the earth and prospers with such guilt on his shoulders is an abomination to me. I want him to fall down and die, in great pain, I think.

"But it is not simply that I am a coward, though I am, that keeps me from trying to stab him to death in his sleep. That is what I suspect he did to Father Gerald. I might yet do it. But this desire, this obsession, of mine is an abomination to me as well. You might call such an act just, but it would offend against everything I want to preach, that I do preach.

"I need to be delivered from this hatred. It sickens me. Yet I feel it every day. And, meanwhile, I go about my tasks. Most often they seem to redound to the benefit of that monster! Riddle me a parable out of that cesspool, Martin."

Martin had never heard his priest friend speak with such passion. He knew that only the dark and their friendship made it possible. It moved him and somehow consoled him about his own problem. Perhaps he would go and try to calm Ermentrude. She was too practical a woman to weep all night.

"Well, for now, Simon, we both will continue to serve the devil. If your God has sent him to us, we don't have much choice, do we? But you will have to pray very hard for your friends—especially your married friends."

Chapter Eleven

The royal encampment had been set up where the monastery of Sahagun abutted most closely on the town. The corrals for the animals of the royal party had been repaired and now stood full. The lowing of the cattle and the whinnying of the horses filled the air while the farmers of the area surrounding the town and some of the lay brothers of the monastery vied for their manure. The smoke of cook fires was constantly in the nostrils and the laughing, chaffering, quarreling voices of men overwhelmed the more subtle sounds of nature.

The pilgrims, some of them, had never seen such a great crowd of men and women nor had Martin. Even those among the band who had come from the large towns of northwestern France had almost forgotten that such scenes existed after the trials of the last three months.

Simon guessed that there must certainly be more than a thousand people, perhaps 1,500, gathered there on the plain of Leon. The party of the king was a small, traveling city in itself. A sizable troupe of drovers, shepherds, and grooms was necessary simply to manage the oxen, horses, mules, sheep, and beef cattle. Then there were the cooks and their helpers, the carters whose oxcarts, empty now, bore the grains, wine tuns, water casks, tents, and armor that served the whole court while it was on the move about the countryside.

Since their arrival, the carpenters and wheelwrights of the crown had been sporadically at work on those carts in danger of losing a wheel or a yoke as a result of the strains of the journey just completed. The court had come down from a trip through the mountains of Galicia to Santiago de Compostela. That had been a hard road and everyone was glad for a holiday from it. To keep up, the blacksmiths and their apprentices had set up their forges and the reshoeing of the more valuable animals was done in train, as was the less pressing repair of bits and pieces of the armor of the assortment of warriors who formed the bodyguard of the king.

The tents had been set up first. The great royal tent itself stood with its extensions on the one side for the monarch's sleeping quarters and for the royal chapel on the other, even though the king would stay most often in the monastery itself. He was so frequent a visitor here that he had added a considerable palace to the monastic complex of Sahagún. But while he would ordinarily attend mass in the monastery church where his father was buried, there was business to be attended which was hardly fit for those sacred precincts. Then he would repair frequently to his own tents to conduct it decently and out of the sight of the lord abbot.

But his French queen, Constance, had her own tent of a size considerable enough to house not just her own person but that of the ladies of her household. When the court had passed through the towns of Astorga and Leon, the bishops of those places had attached themselves to it also. Arrived at Sahagún, their own tents had been set up in as much proximity to the royal ones as could be decently managed. Alerted by some intelligence of important matters to be decided, the bishop of Oviedo had hastened down over the mountains from Asturias as well and his tent blossomed next to the others. Then there were the smaller, more weather-beaten tents of the king's majordomo, his standard bearer, and three of the great counts of the realm just now in attendence upon him.

What Simon, Martin, and Ermentrude beheld was a combination of city bustle, country fair, and social pageant spread in gorgeous panoply over the dry plain about the tiny River Cea, now hardly more than a rivulet in the heat of full summer. Then there was the backdrop of the humbler encampments of the pilgrims. Two bands preceding Rainald's were still held enthralled by the excitement of the occasion when they themselves had arrived. Another pilgrimage had followed them in this morning. The camps of the pilgrims looked and smelled much like those of the hangers-on, casual travelers, merchants, whores, supplicants, and runaways, who had come in on the flanks of the royal party.

The trio would have examined the scene at some greater length but Rainald hurried them along. Finally Simon detached himself on the plea of attending services at the monastery church which they were now passing. Like many others that they had passed on their journey, it had about it bits of scaffolding, mounds of worked and unworked stone, and the huts of the masons who had taken up more or less permanent residence for the duration of their building project. Rainald was quite willing that Simon should leave them. The knight had not wanted the priest to tag along with them in the first place. There might even have been trouble then but the king had brought his peace along with him and casual violence was therefore a dangerous indulgence, even for the mighty, so long as the person of the monarch remained in this place.

Rid of the cleric, Rainald hastened Martin and Ermentrude along even more. His objective was a row of stalls and tents leaning more or less permanently against the wall of the town.

Ignoring the whines of the merchants and beggars, the knight led Martin and Ermentrude to a tent close to the end of the row where a proprietor, one-armed and clad in a truly vile and wonderful assortment of rags, stood and bowed repeatedly at his approach.

"You, thief! I will need a suitable tunic and boots for my groom here. Something that will not embarrass me if he were to follow me into the presence of the king himself. I will not haggle with you about price but think twice before trying to cheat me. You and I both know that the true owners are still looking for their stolen garments—that is if your cutpurses even left them their lives."

The man blinked furiously. Rainald had spoken to him in his native French and he understood perfectly. There was something cold and hard about this pretty young man which would make bargaining perilous. He mumbled and bowed. Then he turned to a large, heavily bound chest and, after a moment or two of burrowing into its contents, he straightened up holding a russet tunic.

"This should do for your groom, excellency. It is clean— almost new. The green piping about the armholes and collar is very fine. Just his size. Does he have a suitable belt? I may have one later in the day but not just now."

"Forget the belt, you wretch. I'll not have you murder again just for that. The tunic will do. Now delve again in your pilfered treasury. This time you will find a suitable gown for this lady, my groom's wife. No more than I would have some booby poke fun at the figure of my groom, would I have the lout snicker at the rags and tatters of his woman."

Ermentrude had not expected any of this and she started confusedly at Rainald's words. He quieted her with a slight raise of his hand.

"Do not protest, dear lady. I know what is best for you—

and what is best for your husband. A gentleman should do well by his groom."

The merchants eyes darted between the two. Then he turned again to rummage in his chest. Brief as it was, the encounter between the two chilled him. Nervously he extracted a dress and very carefully held it to her body. With such a woman he might ordinarily have taken some slight liberties in doing so but now he was too nervous to attempt it.

"A splendid dress, my lord. Catch the way the green and gold of it shines for the beholder. A touch of the thread here and there and it will fit the good woman perfectly."

Rainald only half-listened to the man's whining tones while he watched Ermentrude. The poor drab was taken with the garment. He could see that, hard as she might try to conceal it. He found her reactions amusing.

"You do well so far, vulture. Now I will require a pair of boots, good leather not ground to pieces or cracked as your dried streambeds, for the man and leather slippers of the same quality for the woman as well."

"A moment, a moment, my Lord."

The man hobbled furiously down the row to speak to an equally villainous-looking older man before an incredibly dirty tent. They spoke in French but in guarded tones. After a brief but intense spate of exchanges, the old man produced both boots and slippers.

Then it took but another moment or two to complete the business. The clothier asked but half of the figure with which he would have usually begun and Rainald produced from his purse but half again of that figure and dropped it into the man's outstretched hand. The other hesitated for an instant. Perhaps there might be more? Then, thinking better of the least appearance of protest, he began once more to bow repeatedly as he backed away, mouthing his gratitude and promising Martin and Ermentrude eternal satisfaction with their new garments. He had decided that he wanted no more dealings with this knight with the eyes of stone.

Rainald now led his two companions back through the jumble of the tents toward the corrals on the outskirts of the camping area. As they went there was much to see. Women washing clothes and children. Men dicing, mending leather harness, and sharpening weapons. Many of the tent flaps were tied back and stores and possessions could be seen within. The knight was pleased to see that Ermentrude missed most of this though it would usually have engrossed any woman. While Martin had slung his new tunic and boots over his shoulder for ease of carrying, she had folded her dress carefully over her right arm. As she walked, Rainald noticed, she held it high to avoid the refuse and offal of the ground and her eyes strayed to it repeatedly as they progressed. That purchase was going to return its value in entertainment he was sure.

When they reached the corrals, a number of ostlers and their assistants were engaged in moving the stock from the largest of them. As the three watched, some of the rails and poles of the farthest end were knocked down and moved back. Clearly the intent was to double its size. Meanwhile, others were laboring to replace rotted rails and to brace the upright poles all around the new perimeter of the enclosure. Still others were raising the framework for a pavilion to adjoin the corral on the largest level piece of ground.

After watching for a bit, the knight spoke to Martin in an aside.

"These people make the killing of bulls a sport, Martin. That is what they are getting prepared. Tomorrow afternoon any gentleman who thinks that he can kill one with style and grace is welcome to try his nerves and his horse. Their king, Alfonso, and his queen will be here to watch and to award a prize to the best among the horsemen. I intend to enter the competition, to win it, and to be introduced personally to the king. That is why we took our little shopping trip this morning. When the king receives me, I shall need you at hand to attend Julius. Alexander would be a shade too slow for this sort of close work, I think. Beside that, Alexander is such a beautiful, massive brute. The horse should never get more attention than his master, eh?"

Martin had never before seen the knight in something approaching genuine good humor. He was clearly excited at the prospect of the contest and, devoid of his ordinary cynicism for the moment, he seemed simply an attractive and handsome young man. But then the mood passed into Rainald's more usual pose.

"I decided that you should attend me, while I wait on the king, because you at least give the show of some intelligence. More, certainly, than the rest of my men-at-arms do, and especially now that you will be suitably dressed. Ermentrude, for her part, can hold the palfrey's reins. No one who attends should think that I have less than two horses. I will ride the mare but compete on Julius. That little genius will be a revelation to these yokels.

"So we'll display both of them after I win the contest. Julius and you will be right up front—suitably behind me but close enough to dazzle the court, don't you think? Ermentrude will be farther back with the palfrey, but close enough to hand me the reins and let me ride off in style with my award.

"Should I be killed, by any mischance, the two of you may keep the clothing as a reward for your faithful service."

So saying, Rainald turned and made off toward an important-looking Spanish knight. This gentleman was attended by a clerk with wax tablet and stylus. As young knights obviously interested in competing approached him, he engaged them in conversation briefly. To some he shook his head in denial and they strode off in anger and humiliation. In response to the petitions of others, he nodded assent and directed a few words to his clerk who made notations in the wax of his notebook.

"Your pardon, my dear sir, but you must be the master of the games."

The Spaniard turned at this salutation and surveyed the Frenchman with some curiosity. After a moment he replied in good, if stilted, French.

"I am the king's steward, sir knight, and therefore I am the master of everything between the two horizons here."

Rainald was taken aback. He had drawn Martin along after him, expecting to have to depend on his groom to translate. But he recovered rapidly and gracefully.

"And master of the language of we poor French as well, sir steward. I have not expected to find this accomplishment so far from home."

"My good mother was French, sir. I learned the tongue at her knee before I had well learned the Leonese of my father. I take it from your question, and because you chose to approach me, that you have some ambition to compete in our little amusements."

"I would gladly do that if you were to be so kind as to admit me, sir steward. You will see that I am not unskilled at weapons and I should furnish good entertainment to his majesty if given the opportunity to do so."

The steward was a man of full middle age, short but wiry, skin tanned by the sun, with clear black eyes that spoke to the habit of command. He was interested by the Frenchman whom he regarded with some condescension and amusement.

"You may furnish more amusement than you imagine—and in ways that you do not anticipate, friend knight. Have you ever fought a bull from horseback? It takes a range of skills that you and your mount may well learn only tardily—and to your discomfort."

Rainald understood that the other was quite deliberately baiting him. Nevertheless, he controlled his anger as best he could. The steward had the power to deny him the right to compete. Once he had been given the chance to perform, the man would see his mettle soon enough.

"I have chanced my life, sir steward, in amusements much more trivial. Your master would not find me stale or timid game. My stallion, I dare say, could run your bulls to their death if that were the object. I have not so far seen his like, here south of the mountains. His beauty alone would more than repay your master's attention."

His reply, carefully just short of insolence in its delivery and tone, apparently met with the other's approval. The reply was steeled but civil. It brooked no further argument.

"Understand, good knight, that courage is the least of it. We presume that much. Wit and style are much more to the point. Some of the men you may have seen me turn away have tested well already on the field of battle. They too would die well here. But these are games—not wars. It is the doing, not the dying, that is wanted here.

"You will appreciate that you have much to learn by comparison with most of the men who will compete here tomorrow. Still, my mother will be here and she would be pleased to see one of her countrymen in the lists, I'm sure. Then too, the queen is Burgundian herself and might well be interested too.

"As much as I can do then, is to place you as a substitute. I think that I can still promise you some role. As these things go, almost certainly someone's horse will be gored and killed. The man himself may be, if he's really awkward or slow. That leaves a bull that must be dispatched and such will be your opportunity to parade, cockerel. By the time it has arrived, you will have learned something by watching the better fighters. On the other hand, so probably will the bull. Don't ever underestimate one of those brutes.

"That's your chance, sir knight. Shall I have you so listed?"

Rainald understood that he had no further hope. The man had yielded up as much as he was likely to.

"I accept with thanks, my good steward. And I promise you for my part that your royal master will have fair amusement."

Before he could be further patronised by the man and, in the process, run the risk of losing his temper, Rainald turned and walked rapidly away. Before long he slowed, to allow Martin and Ermentrude to come up behind him.

"So you see, Martin, how the great ones of the world manage these things. It is a pity, indeed, that you mulishly refuse the fully free service that you might give me. As my man, you might learn much that, at present, your peasant obstinacy denies you in this life. But I continue to have hopes for you, Martin; I continue to have hopes. It is a long way yet to Santiago de Compostela. A long road teaches much, even humility in the end, don't you think?"

The knight did not really expect a response from his groom. Martin was exasperatingly stubborn. Moreover, the woman had more hold over him than he was likely to admit in the presence of another—or even to recognize himself. But Rainald sensed that the woman begrudged him every service that her husband rendered to him. That made it doubly amusing to offer the man a chance at yet closer service. The man would not accept but the woman would fume at the mere notion. That was clear.

And thus, two disgruntled and one most pleased with himself, they picked their way back to the pilgrim encampment.

Chapter Twelve

The royal pennon stirred listlessly in the late afternoon breeze. Beneath it sat King Alfonso on a raised and richly cushioned chair, taller than many of those around him even while seated. His extraordinary height displayed the black and yellow tunic of León to full effect. The golden orb of kingship resting across his knees was hardly necessary to proclaim his majesty. Curled, bright red hair and a lightly tanned face proclaimed his ancestry in the mountains of the north.

From time to time he turned to his queen for a passing observation, but his attention to the matters in the field never suffered from that courtesy. Queen Constance was clad in the colors of her native Burgundy for the day's festivities, her deep green eyes glistened with excitement, and her honey-colored hair fell in cascades dressed with jewels. The royal pair made a brilliant match. The presence of three bishops, half a dozen abbots, and twice again as many counts and nobles, all of them clad to impress the king as well as one another, failed utterly to dim the glory of the royal couple.

There was much polite jostling around the improvised throne and a considerable amount of noise as the members of the court differed with one another on this or that matter, hoping thereby to gain the momentary attention of Alfonso. The king was oblivious to none of this, though he had long known that a decent reserve protected him best against these constantly threatened importunities. He was careful to bestow his attentions very rarely and then only in passing. Consequently, he was the first of them to react to the sudden turn of events in the corral.

A young Asturian had been, he thought, preparing the bull for the first of the thrusts of the lance that would ultimately slow the brute sufficiently to allow him to be dispatched. But that dun-colored mountain of muscle had, instead, abruptly cut inside the unwary rider's path and hooked a horn behind the right foreleg of his mount. As the great shoulder muscles came into play, horse and rider were hoisted into the air.

In an instant, the man and his mount were in the dust of the corral. The young rider managed to retain enough balance to free his feet from the stirrups as they went down so he was thrown but not caught underneath his horse. The man rolled, scrambled to his feet, and then ran for the corral fence at all the speed he could muster. The crowd cheered for the bull and jeered after the man, laughing at first as they shouted insults. The rider was safe enough. He had landed with his mount between him and the bull. That great animal now began to savage the steed, hooking it again and again in his fury. From the first, the horse had been unable to rise. It lay bleeding more copiously each instant and screaming in pain and terror.

Almost immediately, the mood of the spectators changed and they began to hoot at the hapless young man in their sympathy for his mount. As he attempted to climb the corral fence, some of those nearby struck at him with staves, pushing him back into the arena. They formed a wall along that barrier, making it impossible for him to escape.

And already the royal steward by the gate had turned to

Rainald. "Your moment now, cockerel. See what you can make out of that fool's mess and do it quickly. The king has a feeling for horseflesh and this is ugly, God knows."

As the corral gate was swung back, Rainald urged Julius slowly into the enclosure. He kept his mount at tight rein, and angled his approach so that the stallion had to step nearly sideways as it approached the horse from the side opposite the plunging bull. It was a pretty exhibition of horsemanship, given the screams of the horse and the profusion and smell of blood. If the bull failed to catch sight of his new adversary, the crowd's attention was secured soon enough. Fascinated by this new play, they lost interest in the defeated rider who finally managed his exit from the scene of his humiliation.

Virtually atop the fallen horse and its attacker, Rainald reined up Julius entirely. For a moment he surveyed the tangle. Then a swift lance thrust cut the poor horse's struggles abruptly. Its screams stopped. After a convulsive jerk of legs and hooves, it lay quite still.

In confusion at the change in its prey, the bull backed away. The great head swung from side to side. Only then did the massive animal perceive the presence of the new horse and rider.

Hooting and waving a glove, the knight made doubly sure that he had the animal's attention. Then he began to let Julius canter away from the dead horse, drawing the bull along with him. Gradually the new adversaries increased their speed. Keeping always to the left of those massive horns, employing the fleetness of the more nimble Julius, Rainald kept just out of reach of the furious animal as he led him in a series of long arcs, the bull almost touching the fencing of the corral.

The crowd moved back from those railings. The bull was capable of either jumping or simply breaking through them if this golden-maned youth lost control of him and everyone understood that. But Rainald never did lose command of the creature. Around and around in that arena he led the great beast, with the dead horse in the center. When the bull stopped, lungs gasping, he and Julius danced prettily back to it, only to wheel away when it renewed its charge. When it hesitated too long, the knight put the spurs to his stallion a moment before he reached in with his lance and thrust into the great muscles of the beast's shoulders. Stung into motion, the bull resumed its charge only to find its opponent again just out of reach. Again it was led about the corral, panting and gasping but now bleeding as well.

Struck by the control of the man and the unerring response of his stallion, gradually the crowd fell more and more quiet. In the afternoon sun, the jingle of metal, the hooting of Rainald, the panting of the bull, and the alternating pounding of hooves, formed a pattern of sound that rose and fell in a rhythm that spelled death to the one or to the other. The circle of blood around the edges of the corral thickened and deepened.

Now the bull turned wearily away from another futile chase. In its near exhaustion, the animal failed to mark that the man and mount had turned behind him. Before he could react, the two had become a single projectile. With the combined weight of himself and Julius, the knight leaned forward in the stirrups and plunged his spear deep into its loins, forward of the hips. The bull bellowed and staggered. It lost control of its hind legs and fell to one side, scrabbling with it forelegs in a vain effort to stand. The butt of the knight's spear swung in agitated circles in the tissue just before its hindquarters.

Rainald had reined up Julius in front of the stricken animal and paused for some moments to survey the effect of this last tactic. Then he dismounted, sword drawn. Leaving the stallion to hold the bull's attention, he walked warily and wide around the horns until he was behind the great head. Then, with a great, arcing swing, the sword came down on the neck of the beast. Its forelegs drove, the massive neck strained with the horns, but the damage had been done. Choosing his time, again the knight stepped in and again the sword bit into the neck. The pattern had to be repeated three times, but finally the head sagged to the ground, the great blue-white vertebrae of its neck exposed and shattered.

A long note from the trumpet drifted out upon the early evening air, signaling the end to the games and the summoning of the contestants to the presence of the king. Three native knights who had preceded Rainald on the field were greeted in turn by their ruler with fair comments upon their performances. Then the royal chamberlain bestowed a small purse of coins on each and they stood aside from the throng of the court to observe the remainder of the ceremonies.

The royal steward and master of the games himself led Rainald forward. The other knights obviously had been no strangers to Alfonso, but Rainald had to be presented to him properly. The knight had surrendered Julius's reins to Martin, who now stood with Ermentrude on the outskirts of that growing crowd. Their master noted with satisfaction that, in their new clothing, they made as good or better a show than other folk of the lesser sort who were also pressing in about the royal party. They would be quietly noticed by these simpering courtiers. He did wish that Martin had made a fairer choice than the plain Ermentrude, but the woman did glow, just a bit, with her pride in her man, with her satisfaction with her new garments, and her excitement at the royal presence.

"Majesty, this young gentleman, Rainald of Poitiers, whom you have just seen kill the final bull, is a Frenchman of good family. He is here in your realm with a pilgrimage to Santiago de Compostela, which he leads. His mounts spoke to his quality and moved me to allow him to chance participation in the games if someone else should fail or be unable to play his assigned part. I trust that your majesty has been pleased with our choice."

"As usual, Rodrigo, your choice has been unerring in its ability to interest us. As you know, we are always interested to welcome the French to our kingdom."

Alfonso said this with a slight smile—and a sidelong glance at his steward's mother, standing among the ladies of his queen, Constance. Then he turned to Rainald.

The king was at least a head taller than the knight. He was also two decades his senior, and carrying some of the weight that accumulates even with the most active maturity. But his vigor and the force of his person reinforced his royal status and made an almost physical impact on those whom he bestowed his full attention. Rainald felt it now. The slighter and shorter, blond youth instinctively bridled somewhat at this unavoidable pressure on his self-esteem.

The two, from the first, were prepared to dislike one another. Both were aware instantly of the other's reaction, however much they chose to dissimulate it on such a public occasion.

"Welcome to our kingdom, young gentleman of France. We are always pleased to receive countrymen of our queen. We are especially pleased when they afford us such pretty entertainment. That is a splendid stallion that you ride. There are bigger horses perhaps, indeed I am told that you sometimes ride one such, but this horse is both shapely and superbly trained."

"Thank you, your majesty. I appreciate the hospitality that you have afforded me and the opportunity that your steward provided to ride and fight a little before your royal presence.

"My stallion, Julius, is small as his breed goes, but of an excellence beyond his stature, as you have seen. I personally trained him. But of course, one chooses a mount for the purpose at hand. For a modest encounter, a modest steed. However, I would be pleased to make a gift of him to your majesty. Put to stud, he would surely enrich the royal herds."

There was a stir among the nobles surrounding the king at the boldness of the man's words. Rainald turned slightly, so that Martin could see him clearly and understand his purpose, should he not have heard the exchange. The latter led Julius forward a bit, just to the edge of the royal party. Under a tight rein, the horse showed prettily indeed and Alfonso's eyes betrayed his frank appreciation of its worth.

"You make a gallant offer, young man, to be sure. But I would be loath to impoverish such a good young gentleman. Surely you will have need of this Julius to accomplish your vows. The road between here and the shrine of Santiago is long and your company seems small. But for the sturdy groom here, I am told that you are attended by merely four other men-at-arms. Still, it may be the practice of your countrymen to limit their attendants out of respect for the pious nature of the enterprise."

Rainald blushed. Martin, thank God, had presence enough of mind to gradually withdraw the horse upon the king's refusal of it. The knight could not entirely contain his fury at this humiliation, yet he understood the need for care. Hospitality had it limits.

"Your majesty is honored by your solicitude for a knight traveling foreign lands. I must own the number of my men-at-arms was larger before we were set upon by bandits, more than once, here south of the mountains. With your permission, I will recruit replacements for them among the local populace before going on. As for the stallion, as you know I have another, a larger one, though not so finely nerved perhaps as the one your majesty has seen fit to return to me."

Alfonso continued to smile easily. This puppy had some self-control, for all of his visible stiffening on being rebuked. And the man was a superb horseman.

"You have our permission to recruit a further following. I regret that your party should have been so roughly handled in our land until now. A good commander bleeds for his men. When you have fulfilled your vows, sir knight, you might consider our service as a rewarding way to employ your new freedom. We will have use, shortly, for as many as have a taste for a more exacting field.

"For the present, we thank you for the entertainment of the afternoon. Your skills as horseman are of a high order, for sure. If you have something yet to learn about the technique of slaying a bull with grace, that is to be expected of one so newly come to our land. However, we now have no fewer than four bulls to consume this evening. You have our leave to invite your whole company to the repast shortly to be provided to all here present."

The royal chamberlain understood immediately that this interview had ended. A small purse found itself in the royal hands. Alfonso extended it to Rainald who bowed slightly and accepted it with further murmurs of thanks. The king turned away and the royal court trailed off after him.

The feasting had been fulsome. Bellies accustomed to slim and plain fare were stuffed and groaning. There would be vomiting in plenty shortly. Martin and Ermentrude chose to leave before those usual dregs dimmed the luster of the day's festivities. The last two days had been ones of wonder for simple folk like themselves and they had much to occupy their hearts and their tongues as they strolled into the dark beyond the fires of the royal campgrounds.

There was the matter, too, of care for their new clothing. Neither one of them could take their good fortune for granted. The richness of their garments demanded care. Attention was necessary as to where they placed their feet in a gathering so great as this. Men and animals relieved themselves where they might.

They were headed for the pilgrim camp, on the far side of the town, well away from the monastery and the royal encampment. A bustle marked the main gate of the town of Sahagún which was being prepared to close for the night. It would have been closed at sundown were it not for the festivities which had detained many of the burghers who could not be shut out of their own town without trouble resulting for some watchman.

Beyond the gate, the line of stalls began with the one where their new finery had been purchased just a day ago. The shops were silent now and leaned in shadows against the town wall in scarecrow shapes, awnings as well as goods safely stowed somewhere in the recesses of the town within the wall.

When the shadows sprang into violent movement, Martin was taken unaware and felt himself flung hard against the wall in a recess between two stalls. He opened his mouth to shout a protest but someone stuck a knifeblade into it, almost to the back of his throat. In terror he was still. Two muffled shapes held his arms—one at each. The knifeman in front fumbled with the belt of Martin's tunic, preparing to draw the garment up over his head. When he removes the knife, Martin thought, I'll have a chance to do something perhaps. But what?

"Don't tear the cloth, for Christ's sake. This one's not going anywhere. Take a little time and get it off whole and unbloodied. Don't make a fuss, stranger. You'll live longer that way."

Martin could guess from the scuffling sounds quite near that another pair had seized Ermentrude. They must have stuffed a gag in her mouth to keep her quiet. Either that, or she was mute with fear—like himself.

There was a low laugh.

"Well, look at this. The gown came off in one piece. Not a rip. That'll bring a pretty price."

"Yes, but the bitch beneath it is old and dry. Look at the dugs. No milk in them for many a year."

"Well, count your luck, friend. If she had been a young one, she might have been in her flowers, all nastiness and blood, you know."

"By God, she'll bleed soon enough anyway when I get through with her."

Martin knew that he must find a way to break free. But he could taste the steel in his mouth and he understood that his life was forfeit if he made the slightest sound or movement.

Suddenly, there was blood all over. It was warm and pulsing and flowed in jets against his face. The farmer in him told him what it was by the smell. The knife came away, cutting the side of his mouth.

"Aaugh!"

It was not his own blood. The figure in front of him was collapsing, clutching at his own throat. Holding his life in with both hands, blood spouting between the fingers.

"What a pretty game! You should have invited me, gentlemen."

The voice was Rainald's, of course. The hands at Martin's arms released and another of the shadowy figures gasped three times in rapid succession. Each gasp succeeded the sound of a blade puncturing flesh. One knew the sound from the butchering each fall on the farm.

Then there was a flash of sparks—and the quick rasp of steel on steel. A scream followed with hardly a pause and the pounding of fleeing feet came immediately after. The thieves could not have expected a knight practised in arms. They had been in search of simpler prey.

Martin and the knight, out of the shadows of the stalls now, could see Ermentrude, nude and swaying. Her assailants had fled without coming to the aid of their fellows or even having been assaulted by the knight. Perhaps they had been unnerved by the way in which he had simply ignored them.

But they had fled without their prize. The Flemish woman still held her gown, a corner of it wrapped around her great fist and the remainder trailing on the ground. She had risked her life to keep it.

"Be so good, woman, as to cover your nakedness. We are, after all, good Christian pilgrims. Carnal delights are what we flee all this long journey."

Martin moved to place himself between Rainald and the woman. Ermentrude managed to control her trembling, gather up the dress, and pass it over her head. Anger at the raillery of the knight helped to keep her shock and faintness at bay for the moment.

Rainald was pushing his dagger in and out of the soft ground. It would not do to have a good blade filthy.

"The two of you are no better than children. You are ninnies, no less. Do you know no better than to walk so carelessly near the night shadows in a strange town? If I had not happened along, the two of you would be stiff and cold by now, the fine clothes which I so kindly purchased for you stuffed in some thief's sack.

"You at least, Martin, should have been on your guard. You are my groom, my trail boss, my sometimes man-at-arms. Really, yours was a disgraceful performance."

"He is a man of peace, sir knight. He is a good man—not a

brawling soldier, part brute and part bully. Martin does not see the whole world as enemy."

Ermentrude had lashed out while her husband remained silent. Martin himself felt the justice of what Rainald had said. He had been a fool. But his wife, trembling though she was, would brook no criticism of him from this sardonic killer.

"So much the worse for him, lady. And so much the worse for you as well. The world is as it is, and whoever does not see that will bleed for it soon enough. But he should have sense enough at least not to risk his own wife in his folly.

"And you, woman. You have a too-fine sense of your own virtue. You think me a man of blood—and so I am. You two owe your lives to that happy circumstance—and that on more than one occasion now. You live off my protection and just the other day the two of you were quick enough to accept fine clothing purchased from the gains from my proficiency at arms. Martin and you thrive in my shadow and make a good thing of it. It comes strange then that you rail against one who is your benefactor and hug your imagined virtue to your withered, skinny breasts. I tire of it.

"Now come along back to camp, the two of you. You may be a sorry enough couple but you are my people and no one does ill to mine. I see to that."

Chapter Thirteen

Making camp was always more difficult than breaking camp. By the end of the day almost everyone was exhausted. Despite that, the livestock had to be watered, tethered, and fed. Squabbles had to be negotiated over respective places, far from the stock or close to the cookfires, under the shelter of trees or on the available level places. Wood had to be found and gathered and fires started. The carts had to be unloaded. Sometimes hasty repairs had to be made to them. All of these everyday tasks had to be carried out at precisely the wrong time when no one in the entire company wanted to do anything except rest their blistered, sometimes bleeding feet, and their aching bodies. It fell to Martin to supervise this evening ritual and to impose the necessary discipline that got it done without the actual shedding of blood and with the creation of only a minimum number of new feuds and enemies.

Mornings, Martin thought, were blessedly different. Like today, the pilgrims were fresh and willing to hope, against all reasonable hope, that the coming day would be different. They would carry that attitude into the morning for a few hours at least. Unless it was one of those dawns that revealed another nocturnal death of one or more of the travelers worn beyond the night's restoration by the rigors of the months of tramping, the uneven foods, and the unrelenting heat. Then the general mood was dampened and gravediggers had to be selected. The entire party, Rainald excepted, hung about until each hurried service was over. Even then, if the distribution of the goods of the deceased were substantial enough, the good humor of the pilgrims could be recovered.

By this point in the journey, places in the carts for equipment, or belongings that could not be carried, had long been apportioned. Most of the pilgrims accepted such customs as had been worked out. Bedrolls and packs were quickly and easily prepared and shouldered from long practice. People, animals, and carts found their usual place in the line of march without undue urging. The natural optimism of the morning carried most with it until the real heat of the day began.

Martin, of course, was the first to rise—if one did not count those miserable creatures who for one reason or another had been unable to sleep at all the preceding night. He left to Ermentrude the rolling and loading of their few belongings while he attended to the needs of the stallions who were still one of his major concerns. Before their departure from Sahagún, Rainald had recruited a half dozen new men-at-arms. But for two, they were Leonese with some experience at fighting and with considerable knowledge of the terrain that lay before the pilgrims. Two were actually French adventurers of few resources but some skills at arms, cast up in a strange land by some series of misfortunes best left unexamined. They did have some knowledge of horses. That, and the fact that the knight could communicate with them directly, had made it possible for Martin to delegate to them the routine care of the stallions on the march once he had seen to the condition and disposition of those mounts at the day's break.

Returning now from that primal care, Martin was puzzled to see his friend Simon standing uncertainly by the first of the carts. The little priest had recovered the full use of his leg finally, and now usually shared the actual driving of the ox team with Ermentrude. But this morning Martin's wife was nowhere in sight and Simon regarded his friend somberly.

Without question, Martin turned and sought out the place where they had slept that night. He could see, almost immediately, that their bedroll was just as he had left it at dawn and that Ermentrude still lay within it. Suddenly, he felt apprehensive. As he approached, his wife stirred but made no further motion beyond rolling from her side to her back.

"I shall be going no farther with you, husband. I shall not get up again from this place."

He knelt beside her and placed his hand on her brow. There was no heat, no ague there, but instead a dampish sort of cool.

"Could you eat, wife? I could find you a bit of cheese and some olives."

"No, Martin. I should be sick if I tried to eat just now. I'm just weary—weary to death, I think. Just let me lie here for now."

"We can't do that. Everyone is ready to start the day's march. Let me get Simon and the two of us will put you into the bed of the cart. Then you can rest for a while until you begin to feel better."

She opened her eyes, closed until now, and gazed at him with a mixture of affection and exasperation. Her voice was faint.

"Listen to me, husband. Understand me. I am not leaving this place. I can't. In a very little time I shall be dead. I can feel that."

She paused and turned her head away from him. There was a silence between them for a moment. In it, Martin could hear the nearest pilgrims beginning to murmur at the delay. Then, his wife spoke again.

"This little town of León has some French merchants living just outside it. We saw them last evening when we arrived. By now they will have their own cemetery—perhaps their own church. It is a better place than most to be buried. I would be grateful if you would arrange that for me."

"Martin, Martin, the pilgrims are ready to leave. You are delaying the day's march."

It was the knight. Martin had heard the clatter of the approaching hooves of the palfrey and knew that a decision was upon him. He looked into the man's eyes and read there a studied unconcern behind the impatience.

"My wife is not able to continue."

"Well then, put her into the cart. She can ride it as well on her back as on her backside. We have a good day's march before us."

"She will not go, my lord. She believes that she is going to die and she prefers to die here rather than on the road."

Rainald edged the palfrey closer and peered down at Ermentrude whose eyes were again closed. If he managed to keep triumph out of his voice, he yet made no effort to feign sympathy.

"Difficult to the last, woman? First you deprived me of one steward and now you would deprive me of another. You know the rules of the road. Those who can walk, do walk. Those who cannot walk are carted. Those who can't be carted are buried or left."

Her eyes opened and her gaze fixed on the knight. Her voice was low but there was a small note of satisfaction in it.

"I am shortly to be beyond your rules, sir knight. More important, my death will free Martin from your service. He has worked out my debt to you. He is quit of it and you."

Rainald was clearly discomfited by her stubborn resistance. He turned the palfrey away a few paces.

"Martin," he called. When the latter joined him, the knight spoke abruptly and with some heat.

"Get her into the cart, Martin. We have lost enough time already."

"No, my lord. If Ermentrude wishes to die here, she shall have her way on that. You will have to take the pilgrimage on without the two of us. Its rhythms are well set after all this time. The two new men you chose in Sahagún are competent to handle the stallions. I have to care for my wife now."

Martin had spoken evenly and in a low voice. He chose not to meet the knight's eyes. Rainald, when he replied, was clearly angry. His demeanor and voice were like ice.

"Listen to me, Martin. Ermentrude may think that you have paid your debt to me but I will decide that—not her. By my reckoning I have saved your life at least three times over. If you desert me, I will take it just as simply as I have preserved it. Don't try me. You know me better than that after all these weeks."

Still Martin chose not to raise his eyes from the ground. To challenge the man directly would be to court death for sure. The feigned, stubborn incomprehension of the peasant was his best resort.

"I am grateful indeed, my lord, that you saved both my wife's life and my own not three days ago. But you cannot save her now—anymore than I can. The only thing that either of us can do for her is to soften her dying moments and to bury her decently. You cannot tarry for that since the direction of the pilgrimage is yours. Anyway, as husband, the task falls upon me. I will wait out her last hours here, see to her burial in the local cemetery, and then rejoin you."

Rainald stared in anger at the man's lowered head, but his

expression gradually softened to a sort of amusement.

"When I first saw you, Martin, I took you for a peasant. Perhaps you were. Now you have become rather more a kind of villainous advocate—a lawyer—arguing with your betters without seeming to dare so much. I have perhaps taught you better than I intended.

"But, all right. Bury the woman. But don't mistake me. I am not done with you yet. You will rejoin me on the trail after she is safely in the ground or I shall return for you, whether this motley bunch of pilgrims ever gets to Compostela or not. But if you force me to take so much pains to reclaim you, I will see you skinned alive. I promise you that much. Have you ever seen that? You would die very slowly, Martin."

Without waiting for an answer the knight spurred the palfrey, turning toward the head of the column that had begun to lose its order. Seeing his approach the pilgrims hurried back to their places in line. Simon, who had been bending and praying over Ermentrude during the exchange just concluded, stood and hastened up to Martin.

"I have shriven her of her faults, my friend. Nothing much, to be sure, but she feels the better for it. God will be generous with her but, for now, she needs you."

Then the little cleric half-ran and half-trotted to gain the lead cart. He took its reins just as Rainald had started toward it in evident anger. Again, the knight turned off and the entire column began to jolt unevenly into motion.

Martin watched until the last stragglers had cleared the camp area. Then he returned to his wife. She lay just as he had left her. Her eyes were closed again, her body still but for the slight rise and fall of her breasts.

"Ermentrude."

She stirred and opened her eyes. Martin half-knelt beside her.

"You will be safe here. Why don't you try to sleep for a little bit? I'll go into the town and see if I can find a healer or a doctor of some sort."

Ermentrude smiled wanly.

"That would be foolish, husband. I would be dead by the time you returned. Just sit here beside me for these last few moments—where I can look at you and feel your presence. There is nothing more to be done."

"How can you be so sure of that? I know that you are weak. We all are a little so after all this time on the road. But you have no fever. You are not spitting blood or throwing up your food."

He felt a desperation growing in him. There ought to be something that he could do. The idea of just sitting, waiting, and watching her die made him desperate. His own heart sank at the prospect.

"No. I am fortunate. None of those things is happening to me—at least so far. But something in me broke in the middle of the night. I have been tired, terribly tired for days. You were very kind to get me a place in the cart with Simon. He too was kind and good company for me. We talked a great deal, he and I. But even the jolting of the cart hurt me, drained me by the energy it took to resist and to brace against the bumping. That is not the sort of battle that should have meant a pin to a great, strapping farmgirl like myself.

"I am just worn out, husband. There is no strength left in me. I have been fighting this feeling for days and holding myself together by mere stubbornness. But something in me went last night. I don't know what it was but it felt as though some fluid was just draining away inside of me. Now it is gone. There is no way to get it back. It is over."

"Perhaps if I made you a little porridge? Or I boil some water and make a little broth for you?"

"I would not be alive to drink it. Just sit quietly and help me to get through this."

Martin thought that some color was returning to her cheeks. She managed a weak smile and her eyes fixed him.

"Don't be embarrassed, Martin. I shall not ask you to tell me that you love me. I am not afraid to die now. I am ready. You alone have kept me alive for the past two months."

Her words came with an effort. She was short of breath. But her smile lingered and she continued.

"I am a very fortunate woman, husband. Two months ago you saved my life at the risk of your own—and I was a stranger to you. How many men have done so much for a woman—even one of their own family?

"And then you took a foolish, dried-up old virgin into your bed for your wife. A very long time ago I had given up all hope of a man of my own. I knew that I was ugly, too big, too bony. Worse, I had no property. The offers that I did have were not of marriage, as you may well guess, and came mostly from drunks and old men at that.

"So I hugged my pride to my breast and gave up any childish dreams. I decided on this pilgrimage and sold what little I had claim to for this journey. I never expected to go back. Still, I never expected it to be so long either.

"But when I was already almost dead, I found a husband. Or he found me, which is stranger yet. A young man, a handsome man, who took me to wife and made me happy beyond what even a pretty, young girl could have expected. I have been so proud, Martin! In my heart, I have boasted every day that you were my husband! I have loved you so much that I was jealous even of Rainald. You and he talked so often and so long. But it was to my bed that you returned at night!

"You are a good man, Martin. Don't be sad now. God will be good to you. I have asked Simon to pray for you."

The muscles of her jaw tightened and she closed her eyes. Her body was rigid for a moment and then it relaxed again.

Her voice, when it came, was soft and hardly audible.

"I have a new dress. A dress that would make a great lady happy. I shall be buried in it and I shall be the envy of everyone who beholds me. Take my hand, Martin. Take my hand and close your eyes. Look away! I don't want you to see me die."

Helplessly, Martin did as Ermentrude asked. Her hand lay quietly in his for some moments. Then he heard a series of gasps from her and her hand tightened in his own. At the same time, it pushed against his, moving it away slightly. He knew that she was directing him not to look at her with the last of her ebbing strength.

Then there was quiet. Her hand lay perfectly still in his. After a bit he opened his eyes. When they stopped streaming and he could see, he closed hers.

Chapter Fourteen

The old lady with her five eggs had already arrived. She was always the first to the market. As ever, she would take her basket and sit directly in front of his church for the entire day, not moving until the last stall had closed even though she might have disposed of all of her eggs in the first hour. She would watch and sometimes speak to passersby, but she never turned to talk with him. She knew that he was there. Perhaps she felt some obscure guilt at having blocked him off from the direct view of the market.

It really did not matter. Père Jean was confident that his garlic would sell. It was fine, strong garlic and the wives of the little French community always sought it out sooner or later in the day. Meanwhile he could tilt his stool back against the doorpost of his wattle and daub church and dream of the fine, new, stone structure that he had been promised. The butchers had promised it to him. They were French, almost to a man, and prospered in supplying meats to the rash of monasteries and palaces that had come to grace the newly burgeoning town of León.

It had been a stroke of genius for him to realize that the homesick and the nostalgic among them would be powerfully drawn to the patronage of a church dedicated to Saint Martin of Tours. That was not to say that he was not dedicated to that good saint himself. The same French masons, who were just now so busily adding a wing to the monastery of Sahagún, had promised him and Saint Martin a reasonable price for the construction of a church in the new style. To be sure, they were looking for work to carry them through the next winter in the relative comfort of a town like this, once they had finished at the monastery.

The bishop might hold things up a little. Saint Martin's was the first church built outside the walls of the town in the growing French suburb. His eminence was negotiating for a full half rather than the usual tenth of the tithe of faithful of Saint Martin's. He was sure that a new church there would draw people away from the cathedral itself, which was perennially in need of repairs. The builders had made a bad job of that, but they were long since gone and could not be found to set it right.

Still, the bishop would come around, Père Jean was certain. After all, as things stood, the prelate likely suspected that he was getting far less than the tenth of the tithes actually paid now to the old Saint Martin's by the clannish and close-mouthed parishoners of the French suburb. If he settled for a third of the real tithes, the bishop was certain that he would gain more than he realized from the present, grudging arrangement. By the coming fall, therefore, Jean was positive that a deal would have been struck and the company of masons could be engaged. If the weather were not too bad, he might have his new church in time for the celebration of Easter next.

The sight of the man approaching roused the priest from his pleasant reveries. He was a tall man, drawing some kind of litter after him. A rich-looking woolen tunic marked him as a probable servant of an important person. The fellow boasted well made boots, too.

The man turned to avoid a small knot of country folk, and Jean could see that the litter was actually two stout tree limbs. The burden it bore was a body—a woman's body. A belt below her breasts bound the boughs together there and another looped from one ankle to the other, kept the branches from spreading further at the bottom. The priest had seen such makeshift litters before, employed by pedlars and itinerants too poor to own a cart. But to judge by the richness of the gown on the corpse, she had been important enough in life to warrant a better mode of transport. A rough cloth covering her face assured him that she was indeed dead. He rose from his stool as the man, his face grim, approached.

"I have need of your help, priest, to see to the proper burial of my wife. She died early this morning. Our pilgrim band has gone on but I have stayed to see to a decent burial for her."

Well, if the man was not lying, at least they had been married. The morals of these pilgrim folk were often not better than that of stray cats. You might think that they were worried that there would be too little for them to confess properly when they reached Santiago de Compostela. So far as he could see, there were no obvious marks of violence on the corpse. Even so, it could be a bad business.

"Why bring her here, man? Was there no priest in your company? Most pilgrimages bury their own along the road."

"Because this is a French settlement. My wife was French— from the north there—and she wanted to be buried among her own countrymen. You don't have to be worried about it, priest. She was a free woman. We were married by the priest among our pilgrims and she was shriven of her sins by him before he left. I can pay."

Jean looked more closely at the man. He was obviously a country person from the roughness of his speech but the grief in his voice seemed to be genuine. He spoke in some sort of border patois.

"Where is your home, pilgrim?"

"I come from the Comminges. I left a farm there to come on pilgrimage. My name is Martin. Like your church."

A Frenchman named Martin! Was the man lying? Still, it could be a sign.

"There is a grave already open, stranger. The thief that it was meant for was pardoned by the bishop at the last moment. But he was a little runt and your wife was a tall woman. She would never fit. We would have to hire a couple of men to enlarge it."

"Find them and put them to work, Père. They can finish it while you say the Mass."

"A Mass? Masses are expensive, my friend. This is market day and matters here require my attention."

The man before him kept his temper with an obvious effort.

"Look you, priest. I can pay for your gravediggers. I can pay for your Mass. You needn't worry about any of that. But I need to have this business done with. For the love of Christ, we need your help."

Well, the boy could look after the garlic while he said the Mass. The brat was about somewhere. And the woman! Where was the woman? Off gossiping with the other crones likely. The boy could fetch her. She could at least light the candles without setting the church afire. The old candles would do. There was a finger or so left to them and the man would not care. But the woman was never about when he had need of her. She was more aggravation than she was worth.

"Fair enough, my son. You can move your wife inside still on the litter."

He moved the stool aside and pushed the door ajar.

"Mine is a humble church but there is room enough, I think,

for her. Take her inside—away from these gaping yokels. It will take me a few moments to make the arrangements but she will have her Mass before the morning is done."

Martin rose and stretched. He was unsteady in his purpose as well as on his feet. His food had given out the day before. Four days and three nights he had passed, never more than a pace or two from Ermentrude's grave. She had been buried in the gown of which she had been so proud and the worth of it was a danger. Not a few of the local vagrants would have been eager to dig her up for it. Now, after this length of time in the ground and next to her body, it would not any longer be worth the effort or the risk to them. He was free to go.

The people of the neighborhood regarded him with curiosity as he went. He had come from the pilgrim camp with his unusual burden. He had kept his peculiar vigil, speaking to no one. Even the prostitutes at night who had tested his intentions found him unresponsive. Now as well he spoke to no one but found his way to the city gate and passed through it.

Beyond that portal he became a complete unknown. He was worth a glance and no more. The night was coming on and everyone had a shop to close or a mess of porridge to eat.

At the turn of a street Martin found a woman sitting in the doorway of her home, talking to a boy. She watched him, suspicious as he approached her.

"Can you part with a bit of bread, mother? I can pay for a little food if you can spare it."

She gave him a long look. In the mountains of his home, and on the long journey of the pilgrimage, Martin had picked up a little of the language. Although the woman could understand him, she knew he was no native. After a moment of uncertainty, she spoke a few words to the boy who then disappeared briefly into the house. He was back quickly and dropped six or seven olives into her hand and stood there with a rag half-wrapped about an end of bread.

The woman now looked her question at him without speaking. Martin in turn produced a small leather purse from beneath his tunic and shook two pennies from it. The other smiled a little cautiously. She knew as well as he did that it was generous for what she offered. Perhaps the stranger was going to clip them, or to ask for yet something else. But he didn't. He merely dropped them into her hand, took the proffered bread and olives, and turned away.

When Martin reached the cathedral, he walked around it to the back. There it almost joined the town wall, next to yet another gate. In the angle, formed by a chapel of the apse and deep within the shadows of the wall, he sat and settled his back. Then he began to eat slowly.

The old man joined him almost at once. The rags of his clothing were filthy and the gaping rents in them flaunted a body yet as dirty again. The man's hair stood out at all angles and his eyes were a mix of blood and yellow film. A great, purple nose overhung a mouth entirely without teeth, as far as Martin could see.

The creature said nothing. He merely squatted wordlessly and regarded the seated other. After watching him eat a little, the man extended his hand in supplication but still silent. Martin surveyed him more closely and then gave the old fellow a half of what remained of his bread. The beggar broke it into smaller pieces and began to gum them slowly. The two watched each other as they finished their meager meal. There was business to be conducted here and both knew it.

"We need a skin of wine," Martin said.

"We need two skins of wine."

"One will be enough to start. I have the money. Do you know where you can find one at this time of evening?"

"With money, one can find a full wineskin anywhere, day or night."

Martin handed the old man three coins. If he'd given him enough for two skins there would have been no surety that he would ever see the old drunk again. This way, the man would come back, at least with the first skin if he could find one. While they drank it together, he could take the other's measure and try to determine just how far he could trust him.

His new friend shuffled off with as much speed as he could manage while Martin sat in the gathering twilight. Left to himself, the mild satisfaction produced by the first food in two days gradually ebbed. He thought of the woman's death and how calmly she had accepted it at the last. She had been a brave woman, grateful for the precious little that God had seen fit to grant her. But then, so all three of his wives had been—and it hadn't helped them a bit. Why had he himself been so lucky and the three of them struck down without mercy?

The old man materialized then, out of the dark, bearing the precious wineskin. When he proffered it, it felt a little light, a little too limp, to Martin. Although now he could not see in the dark, he seemed to catch the smell of fresh wine from the man's direction.

"I paid for a full skin, old man."

"And you might have gotten your own, if you'd known where. A porter gets paid, even if he's not a friend."

"All right. All right. Sit down here and tell me your name, you old drunk."

"My name is Pedro. Half the people in this land are named Pedro. Probably their mothers can't think of anything better. Anyway, that's a piece of knowledge that'll get you nowhere—so you can have it for the price of a drink."

Martin handed him back the skin and listened to him suck on it long and deeply. Finally, the man returned it.

"How about you, farmer? You're a stranger looking to get drunk in a strange land. That's bad business—dangerous business. Even worse, you're carrying more than the price of a full wineskin on you. Where do they make such damn fools to wander the highway? Or did you steal that purse from someone else and run off to avoid the law?"

"I had a farm back in the Comminges. It's over the mountains in Frankland. I sold it off to go on pilgrimage. But how did you guess that I used to be a farmer?"

Martin sensed rather than saw the man reaching for the wine again. He took a long drink himself and then passed it to him. His reply was a substantial drink in coming.

"Any fool can tell a farmer by his hands. They're always big, rough, mostly broken hands. Just because I'm a drunk it doesn't mean that I'm stupid. I may be a drunk just because I'm smarter than most. And I know where the Comminges is too.

"You, on the other hand, can't be all that bright. Selling the farm, selling any farm, is a good idea. All farms do is work their owners to death. But going on pilgrimage is a rotten one. There are better ways to die than by walking your legs off. Or did you find that out? Where's your pilgrimage now?"

"It left four days ago. I stayed behind to bury my wife."

There was a short silence. Without being asked, the man handed him back the wineskin. Despite the substance of what he said next, the old drunk's voice was somewhat less sharp.

"No place for a woman, a pilgrimage. You shouldn't have involved her in your stupid piety. Women die easily enough at home as it is. I hope she wasn't pregnant as well."

"I wouldn't have taken a wife on a pilgrimage, old man. I wouldn't have gone on one myself if I'd had a living wife. She had joined the pilgrimage well before me, and we met after the first band I was traveling with turned back and I fell in with hers."

Martin was confounded. The first question the man asked was the one he had never thought to ask himself.

"I never thought about it but I don't think that she was pregnant. For one thing, she was probably too old for that. At least, I think she was. She would have said something if she had thought she was carrying, wouldn't she?"

The darkness in the shadows of the wall was so intense now that neither man could see the other at all. That made the growing familiarity easier for Martin. It added to the careless camaraderie that flows out of a wineskin with the wine itself. Doubtless, even the old drunk would have been more careful of his words without the protection afforded by both.

"Jesus Christ, my friend. What is your name anyway?"

"Martin."

"Martin, you are so dumb that you probably have to use two hands to wipe your own ass. You marry an old woman that you met on a pilgrimage. Did she have money? She dies—and you are not even sure whether or not she was pregnant? Are you a drunk or a lunatic, my friend? No sober, stolid farmer-type behaves like that."

Even though the wine was beginning to make him warm and at ease, Martin felt the need to defend himself. He took another long drink and passed the skin to keep the old man's mouth shut for a bit.

"Pedro, the philosopher! What do you know of the world of sober people? When was the last time that you even saw it?

"The woman had killed a man and was about to be hanged. I went surety for her because I felt sorry for her. Then, as time went on, everyone thought that I was entitled to bed her, even if I hadn't intended to at first. Most of them thought that I had. Hell, even Ermentrude herself expected me to take her, use her, and was ashamed and angry because I didn't. She thought that I thought that I was too good for her!

"Finally, I had no choice but to bed her. She wanted that to keep her pride. The rest expected it. At the very least, I had to show her that she was not so ugly as she thought and to show the others that I had a normal man's desires. But I married her afterwards. There was a priest, a friend of mine, with the pilgrimage."

Pedro was making strangling noises in the dark. At first, Martin thought that the old drunk's haste to finish the wine was going to kill him. Then he realized the man was trying to silence laughter. But he could not. Then he choked indeed—and Martin could imagine the wine pouring out of that rheumy beak of a nose. At last there was silence.

"We need another skin."

The man's voice was subdued. Perhaps he thought that his new friend's anger would deny him that elemental need. But Martin was happy to fumble coins into the outstretched hand. As much as the wine itself, for the moment he desired relief from the drunk's person.

In the latter's immediate absence, he began to doze, back against the stone of the apse. At once, the relaxation made him aware of a slight vertigo and a certain queasiness in his largely empty stomach. Maybe he should have asked Pedro if he could find some food as well. Then again, his stomach might not hold food down. He knew that he was more than a little drunk but put the knowledge away from him angrily. He was entitled to be drunk if he cared to be, wasn't he?

After a bit, he smiled to himself in the dark and even chuckled a little. It was peaceful just to rest here. If the world had begun to whirl around slightly, why should he care? In this state of mind, he was rejoined by his friend with another wineskin. Promptly, they shared another drink.

"Martin, you're a hero. You went to that woman's rescue and you didn't know a thing about her." Pedro giggled. "Then you married her because you didn't want to hurt her feelings. You don't know the first damned thing about women, my friend, but you're a hero. Do you go about the land rescuing them all and then letting them bully you for thanks?"

"You don't know as much as you think you do, you old drunk. I've been married twice before—to young, beautiful women. My Claire was the first. God, she was beautiful. I used to raise her, naked, in my arms, caress her, and cover every part of her body with kisses—until she was panting for me to enter her. Therese, my second wife, was almost as lovely and even more lively. It was she who caressed and kissed me—the whole length of my frame—as we lay and mingled. Don't tell me about women, my friend Pedro."

"Well then, so you were a great lover. What happened to these beautiful paramours of yours, Martin?"

"They died. Claire died in childbirth. Therese was gored by our own bull. Then I was left alone. Now I'm alone again."

Martin could feel his eyes misting. He felt as though he might cry like a child. He couldn't do that! Pedro might jeer at him even if the old fool did want more wine. But it was all so sad. Now Ermentrude had died and he was alone again. He felt the wineskin being pressed upon him once more.

"Here, take it, my friend. Take a long draught. You have been badly used and you deserve consolation. What you have in your hands now is the surest friend you will ever have. The wine is always there. It will outlast both of us."

But Martin could already feel the old man tugging at the skin. He held it tighter and poured it into himself faster but his grasp slipped and the wine trailed over his skin as his companion dragged the vessel away.

He wasn't angry though. Pedro was his friend. He could

have it. Where was he. There somewhere in the dark. The wall against his back was whirling. He fell away—into a deep, deep pit. If it had a bottom . . .

Chapter Fifteen

The bells! The bells! Right above him someone was pulling on those damned bells. Their peals struck sparks that darted about in his head. Ribbons of pain ran deep into his brain. The ribbons swelled, twined, and formed a net that tightened and pressed until he could not think. Cautiously, Martin raised one hand to his head. It was not broken. It was not bleeding. But it smarted to his lightest touch. At last the reverberations of the church bells sank away into silence.

In the quiet that followed, he became conscious of the stench. His stomach roiled at the strength of it. Carefully, he opened his eyes. His lids were caked. He could see the wall of the cathedral, rising stark above him. He moved his head and it caused violent spikes of pain to run along his temples and down the back of his neck. He closed his eyes again and lay very still.

In the brief moment of vision, he discovered the source of the smell. He was lying in vomit, it was all around him—at least he thought it was. Gradually he became aware of the sour taste of his mouth and realized it was his own vomit. He was lying in his own filth.

When had he begun to retch? He could remember drinking with the old man—with Pedro. He could not remember when they had stopped drinking. When had he gone to sleep? He could not remember getting sick. What else might have happened?

Martin rolled on his side—away from the mess. Then he inched himself up until he had his back against the wall. Even such a small effort set his head to pounding and, for a moment or two, he felt that he was going to be sick again. He strained to control his stomach muscles. When the knotting subsided he opened his eyes.

"Waking up is the bad time."

Pedro faced him, sitting on his haunches. Could the old man have gotten dirtier—uglier? Martin watched as the other scratched and belched. The dirt seemed part of the man. It appeared to be what held him together. But the eyes were bright and, just now, they held Martin fast and surveyed him bit by bit.

"You don't look so good yourself, farmer. Don't rush things. It will get better if you take it slow. No sudden movements."

Martin merely grunted. Even that took an effort. Pedro continued to observe him with something between a half-smile and a sneer.

"You'll never make a good drunk, farmer. You're not that close to despair. You think that you are, but you are deceiving yourself. Go back to your pilgrimage."

The man's voice warmed a little.

"You are one of those people who are born serious, Martin. You can't stop hoping. You keep thinking that, if you can find the right thing to do, it will get better. It doesn't; but you keep right on trying.

"No matter how much you bleed, you can't manage to just stop. You can't make up your mind simply to find a way to live the day out. Just surviving until night and the next wine-skin is a trick you'll never learn. I know. I'm the master."

Pedro stood up. It was a remarkable sight. Somehow the clothes held together. They, and the man within, shifted, then settled, and assumed a disarray that yet had a pattern to it. Or this is a nightmare, Martin thought.

"Go back to your own, farmer. You will anyway, sooner or later. That is, if someone like me doesn't cut your throat first. It would be easy enough to do."

Without asking for permission, or speaking at all, the old drunk picked up the wineskins. They could be resold—or traded. Then he walked off around the corner of the cathedral.

Martin watched him go in silence. Then, very gingerly, he pushed himself upright, by half-climbing, half-leaning against the rough cathedral wall. The motion woke the pain in his head that had subsided while he had been quiet. It was so intense that he involuntarily shut his eyes. That action brought on a dizziness so severe that only his grip on the wall kept him from falling.

"Damn."

Carefully he waited until his head had quieted once more. Then he surveyed his immediate surroundings. His blanketroll was still there in its thongs. It had not been stolen in the night, although he had been far too drunk to make use of it. Hopefully, his few portable belongings were still inside then. That thought led him to feel under his tunic for his money pouch. It too was still on his person. From the heft of it, nothing much could be missing. Whatever else Pedro was, he was not a thief.

Tentatively, Martin bent to retrieve his blanketroll. Having managed that successfully, he began to walk, steadying himself by pressing his right hand against the cathedral's wall.

"I'll have to find a stick of some kind."

But he didn't. The grounds about the cathedral were innocent of anything but stones and dust. It was a hard summer. Nothing grew without constant care and there remained nothing that fell over, or was dropped, that had not been scavanged. A priest headed into the great church and a couple of masons on their way to some job site regarded this stinking stranger curiously but then showed no further interest. The city was full of the likes of him. They came out every morning from its overhangs and corners looking just like this one.

Martin turned into the street he knew from the previous day, heading for the gate by which he had entered the city. The old lady, the one who had sold him bread last evening, was already sitting outside her house. The morning sun played about her weakly. If the crone found his condition remarkable, with another day's and night's collection of dirt and mixed stains of wine and vomit on his tunic, she said nothing. She watched him as he passed, but watched him in silence.

Already well down the street, Martin heard the slap of bare feet against the packed earth behind him. He stopped and steadied himself, one hand on the nearest doorjamb. The same boy as yesterday drew up even with him. The child said nothing. He merely made a face and threw a rag-covered object at the man before him. Then he turned and ran.

The missile bounced off Martin's chest to land on the street. There, some of the wrapping came away to reveal a fair-sized end of bread. Immediately, the leanest of rats appeared from a hole beneath the house's foundation, contemplating a dash for the morsel. But the man had wit enough to drop his blanketroll between the rat and the bread. It was a young animal and inexperienced. Faced with the man's intention to dispute him, unable quickly to seize on the man's debility, it decided not to make the attempt on the bread and darted back beneath the house.

Deliberately, Martin retrieved the bread and then the blanketroll. He turned to look for the old woman, his benefactor, but she was not to be seen. The boy had disappeared as well. Neither of them, Martin thought, wants more to do with me. Still, the woman knew that she profited roundly from our business last night. He wondered for a moment if she had been the source of the wineskins as well. No matter. She was a good woman. There was no need for her to feed him further but she had done it. Certainly the boy would not have done it. His face had shown what he thought of the idea.

Without challenge, he passed the city gate that had just been opened. The watch eyed him suspiciously but the drunk had no blood on him, just filth. There was no hue and cry. He didn't appear to be in sound enough condition, of mind or body, to have stolen anything. Would that all the drunks without family or possessions would leave León! The city would be the better for it.

The pilgrim passed next through the scatter of huts that constituted the growing French Quarter. At St. Martin's Church the door was ajar but its priest had not yet taken up his station outside. Farther along he neared the rough cemetery that held what was left of Ermentrude. He hesitated there, thought for a moment to look at her grave, then lurched on almost violently.

A short time later he came to the river. Even with the steady runoff from the Cantabrian Mountains to the north, the usual summer drought had much reduced its flow. Martin dropped his blanketroll and tugged off his boots. Then, still wearing his stained and stinking tunic, he waded into the shallow stream in search of a deeper pool adequate to his needs. Near midstream he found one. The water came past his waist and the bottom was thickly strewn with pebbles.

Carefully, he lowered himself into the clear, cool stream. It swallowed his body, then his neck, finally closing over his head. He lay back, resting his whole tortured frame against the sloping sides of the pool. With the drag of his tunic, there was not enough buoyancy in the water to float his weight. Gradually, its cool embrace quieted his aching head and soaked loose the debris of the preceding night. When he could hold his breath no longer, Martin pushed upright against the pebbled slope so that his head just cleared the surface of the water.

There he took breath after deep breath. He lay with his head back, letting the surface currents gently massage the tangled mass of his hair. Above, the blue of the sky was still fresh and vibrant. The sun had not risen far enough to assert its brassy influence and tiny, wooly puffs floated one after the other across his line of vision.

A profound quiet grew in him. The cool, undulating flow relaxed his muscles and soothed the tension of his nerves. The itching, sticky mass that enclosed his body and his tunic dissolved and drained away. Simply to slip below the waters, to take deep swallows out of its coolness, to keep swallowing even after breath had fled seemed so simple.

Why should he not? The church condemned a suicide but perhaps God would forgive a man simply too weary any longer to live. He had rejoiced in the beauty that God had sent him. He had been truly grateful, he thought. Claire, Therese—he had, after all, married them both. He had made them his wives and he had become a proper husband.

He had thought after their deaths that his joy in them had been too forceful, too unrestrained. He had reflected that perhaps God had punished him for the very excess of his pleasures, legitimate though they might have been. Or it might have been that he had been warned by Claire's inability to conceive that a child would be dangerous to her, and he had persisted in a wanton carelessness with her life.

As for Therese, he knew well that his second marriage offended the wishes and the sense of decency of his own father. But in those months after Claire's death, he had been desperate for solace. He had ignored his father's wishes because he had to. When his father had wandered off, old and sick, in protest of what was happening under his roof, the terrible thing was that he had been content to let him go. Actually, he had been quietly pleased with the old man's disappearance. He had told himself that his father would be all right, that he would look for him after a bit. The man should learn his lesson and mind his own business. Later, Martin had told himself that even if he died out there somewhere, it was his father's time. Meanwhile, he had gone on, enjoying Therese to the full, and swelling himself with pride when her belly began to boast the ardor of his love.

But why them? They had suffered and he had survived. He had acknowledged his excess, his sins afterward, surely enough. He had buried them properly and with genuine grief— terrible grief. He had sold the farm of his family. He had taken a vow of pilgrimage and honored it until now at no little cost. Perhaps he had been secretly content with his sorrow. Perhaps he had been just a bit relieved that his own life had been spared and that his suffering consisted only in mourning those cut down?

Wavelets in the stream lapped about his nostrils. Off in the distance, a crow cawed. The sun was well up. It was warming now and its rays danced about on the water's surface.

With Ermentrude, the whole thing had been different. God could not fault him for lust there. He had not wanted the woman. He had not sought her. God knows, there was little enough pleasure in the bony awkwardness of her body. She had wanted him to desire her—and he had made a good pretense. At least, he had thought that he had. Was she ever deceived?

But it was her doing anyway. She had wanted to play the part of the beloved wife. She had wanted to be, even for so little a time, the envy of the other women with the pilgrimage. And where was the blame in that? Many a marriage was built on that sort of dreaming. They had married properly. He had even hoped, for a short while, that the whole change would save her life, that some small portion of affection and a bit of rest from the most grinding portions of the everlasting walking would have restored her health.

Yet God had pursued her. Finally, he had taken Ermentrude's life. Nothing that he, Martin, had done was able to save her. He was fairly sure that the woman had done little to deserve such attention. She was a pilgrim, after all. She was no wanton, to be sure. She was a virgin when he had taken her, despite her age. She had almost no kin. She was kind. If she had killed, it was neither intended nor unjustified in the circumstances.

So what did God want anyway? Her goodness had not saved Ermentrude. If she had died to punish him, then his service, his sense of decency and compassion, was as unacceptable to God as his joy in passion had been.

He had come to the time for decision. Martin fought to empty his mind. He would wait for just a moment or two. Would there be an answer? Would there be a sign?

The silence grew while he waited. Nothing. In the distance, the crow cawed again. What the hell kind of an answer was that?

In anger, he pushed himself upright in the pool. He felt a little better. His stomach had settled—mostly.

Martin waded to the shore. As he approached his blanketroll he started. His boots were gone! What the hell! He should have dropped them on the water side of the blanketroll. Some thief had slid up, behind its cover, and stolen his boots. Now he would have to go back to town and buy some sandals. Did he always have to play the fool?

He sat on the strand while the growing heat of the sun slowly dried his tunic. Despite himself, he did feel better. The stink was gone from him. The throbbing of his head had subsided to a mere threat. He fumbled in the blanket and found the bread the boy had thrown at him. It was old—so he dipped it in the water. Softened so, the crust did not trouble his stomach. As the heat loosened his limbs, Martin began to feel restless. One could not sit about the whole day.

This time, when he passed in front of the little church of Saint Martin, its pastor was on his usual stool in front. Leaning against his doorjamb still, the priest watched the burly Frenchman cross the small square. Without getting up, or even straightening, he could see the stranger as he stopped at a stall propped against the city wall. The proprietor there dealt in leather goods. The cleric noticed that the man's boots were gone and could guess that he was after sandals to replace them.

Père Jean rose and crossed the square. When he arrived, Martin and the leathergoods man were haggling, more or less seriously, about price. The priest waited quietly until the transaction was complete and the buyer had sat in the dust to adjust the straps of the new footwear. He squatted in front of him.

"There will be work here within the week. By then the masons will have arrived from the monastery at Sahagún. Your pilgrimage probably passed there on the road. They're going to rebuild Saint Martin's Church here in stone. It will take a year, even if everything goes right. It won't, of course. There are always problems in building. For a strong man like yourself, one who knows both French and the local language, there will be a job for sure. You would be doing something for your namesake, your saint, as well. It would be good luck as well as a good living."

Martin briefly considered the man and his offer. It was generous. It would be something to do. Maybe it would be lucky for a change. But no.

"You are generous, father. The offer is a fair one. But I must rejoin my pilgrimage. I have not yet fulfilled my vow to Saint James—so Saint Martin will have to wait. Besides, there are people in my band who need me."

Martin was not really sure why he should have said that last. Something to say, an excuse he supposed. With that, he arose and dusted himself. With a smile and a nod to the priest, he swung away.

Chapter Sixteen

They were good sandals. By now they had molded to his feet. A mere two days had passed since he had left León and they had already grown to fit him. The old Roman battlements of Astorga lay off to his southeast now and the mountains rose ahead. He had skirted the city—just as he had avoided the pilgrim bands of the road. They had the usual fear and distrust of a solitary man. Some of the latter had thrown a casual stone in his direction, for he was not so far from them and the road that pointed west. They did not understand a lone traveler who paralleled their journey but pointedly refrained from joining himself to their company.

Martin did not understand it himself. For now, at least, the solitude was comforting. Also his progress was better for he was not impeded with the cares of camp making, or the travails of splintered wagon wheels, or with the business of hurried funerals. For that reason, he had passed several pilgrim bands in just those few days. But, in truth, they all looked much the same. After so many long miles, all were bedraggled, ragtag. There was little in them to attract him, at any rate.

So he found his food through casual contacts with the farmers of the countryside. By now he spoke the language of the land with some ease. The peasants, too, distrusted him but they were in their own element and confident in their combined ability to best him if need be. In fact, he was careful to depart their tiny hamlets well before the onset of the night. It was just possible that they would decide to make an end of the stranger. Such as he could always bring bandits down upon them, though he presented no problem in his single person. So Martin made his night fires small and set them, and his encampments, in spots concealed from ordinary paths and byways.

Now he was concious of the lift of his own spirits. The unending plains behind him had weighed, he guessed, on all of the pilgrims more than any of them had realized. The walking would be harder now and the roads would be worse yet. Food was going to become scarcer and the nights colder. But just now, the change was worth that—and more.

This place had been perfect for the night. A little path that widened into a shelf, difficult of approach from below, but that ran on up the side of the hill above. Martin had learned to distrust anything that smacked of a cul-de-sac. The cliffside overhung just enough to furnish some shelter from rain or dew without constituting a cave that might attract bears.

His modest night fire had long since burned out and no longer even gave off smoke that might draw unwelcome attention to his presence. It had been light for some time now but Martin was loath to leave his bedroll just yet. A pair of hawks soared in deceptively lazy circles in the pale blue of the sky above the narrowing sides of the valley floor. The man guessed that they must have a growing brood of fledglings somewhere to be hunting so early in the day as this.

Watching their effortless motion was pleasant, but he knew that he was prolonging this moment partly to put off rising. Of course his bones ached. Sleeping outside on the ground was a game for younger men than he—and foolish ones at that. He came to his knees and began to fold the bedroll. There had been, he remembered, precious little in the way of slender pine boughs, needles, or leaves with which to stuff it last night. He would have to make more of an effort if he wanted to wake mornings feeling fresher. Hillside camps tended to be safer but they furnished much less in the way of padding.

He arose with his few preparations for departure already complete. His perch overtopped even the tallest mountain pines reaching up from the slopes below and the valley floor with its pilgrim path rising up into the pass ahead. On it he could see evidence that he was not the only one to have slept late this morning. Perhaps a score or so pilgrims were hurrying in some disarray along the track. There were no carts or horses among the group and only one badly overloaded ass, being beaten enthusiastically to increase the beast's willingness to tackle the climb before them at a faster pace.

Martin guessed that this little band properly belonged to a larger company of pilgrims that had gone on ahead in impatience with their morning's delay. Perhaps they had tarried behind intentionally, the better to bury one of their own number. That was the sort of casual disorder that Rainald had never allowed. In the knight's company, no one but the appointed scouts went ahead or followed behind the whole body of the pilgrims. Well, Martin thought, it was more congenial to move at his own pace for now.

Then he realized that he had been half-concious for some minutes of other human noises. He stopped and put down his bedroll. The sounds arose from somewhere not far below him. Cautiously he approached the edge of the shelf and peered over. If they had been quiet, he would never have made them out below among the pines and scrub of the hill. But they themselves were intent on the straggling pilgrims in the valley below and had no reason to be particularly careful.

Clearly they were bandits who had taken up this position before dawn. Martin's hair stood up along the back of his neck as he understood that they now lay in ambush of stragglers such as these. There seemed to be no more than nine or ten of them and they would not have dared an attempt on a larger pilgrim company in daylight. But he could see that they were sufficiently well armed to be able to overmatch the hapless figures spread out on the trail beneath. Even if he would, it was clear to him that he had no way to warn their intended victims. The wind, here on the hillside, was brisk enough so that he doubted that the very loudest of shouts would reach them. Even if they heard, they were likely simply to regard him as a man made mad by the isolation and loneliness of the mountains. He was helpless to avert the impending slaughter.

But perhaps not. Behind him lay the remnants of a small rockslide that had gone no farther than his friendly shelf. He was on them in a moment, prying, heaving, lifting, and tugging free. The larger stones he rolled or tossed to the edge of his perch. He was quick to pile up an adequate trove for his purposes. It had to be done before the brigands below began to slink down the hillside toward their unaware prey. Finally, he could wait no longer.

"Eeeeeiyah! Eeeeeiyah!"

He could hear someone screaming. Then he realized that it was himself.

One after the other, he had begun to hurl the heavy rocks down on the heads of the unsuspecting bandits. One of them was hit. With a shout and a curse, the man dropped his bow to clutch at his shoulder.

There! He'd gotten another one. The point of a sizable stone had caught the man on the head and stretched him out on the ground. As best Martin could see, he was bleeding from the nose and mouth.

No more surprise now. The first rain of missiles had taken them unaware and had given him easy targets. Now the group below was still confused. They had no idea how many their attackers were—or where they might be. But some of them had caught glimpses by now of at least one crazy man on the ledge above them who continued to rain down missiles upon them. They took cover behind those trees that offered the most protection against the hail from above while they peered anxiously in all directions. From what quarter was it most likely that his companions would appear?

Martin was laughing now when his breath permitted, and launching stone after stone as fast as he could find a likely target. But he could not stop to aim very often. The whole point of the attack was to immobilize the men below. Stone after stone ricocheted off tree limbs and trunk. Their targets cowered away from the sounds.

By this time, Martin could not stop himself. He laughed. He shouted curses. The sudden sweat ran into his eyes. Yet all this while, he measured and gauged how rapidly his first stock of stones was running low. Now he was screaming as much in frustration as in battle lust.

"Aauuugh! Aauuugh."

He launched the last few rocks into space. He had to collect more. But even the few feet to the back of the ledge was too much. It would give his adversaries time to collect their wits. It was impossible to hold them much longer.

He darted to the rear of the ledge and seized on four of the handiest and most manageable stones. Then he was back at the edge, shouting anew and seeking any target—even half-visible ones. Speed was the key. Those gone, again he sought the easiest missiles. Again he rushed back to hurl them down.

His throat and chest were pounding now with the exertion. He gulped air in long sobs.

No matter. The men below sensed the change of tempo immediately. The quickest of them had guessed by now that there was but one man up above them on the ledge. More than that. Their tormentor might be entirely alone. No other had shown himself. The only danger that had materialized was the hail of rocks. No arrow had been launched. There was no sound of sword on shield.

Tentatively at first, they began to concentrate on the man on the ledge. Those with bows nocked arrows and waited for a glimpse of him. Martin had known that such a reaction was inevitable. He began now to choose spots from which to throw as varied as the small reaches of his perch allowed. To aim was increasingly difficult. Some arrows climbed toward him even so. They missed. But the aim would improve. Time was running out.

The bandits below had just about become convinced that they had only one man—a crazed hermit or shepherd perhaps—with whom to deal. Cautiously at first, then made brave by growing certainty, some of them sought to find the way up to the ledge.

Others caught sight, almost at the same moment as Martin himself, of the change that was taking place on the valley floor. Some trick of the wind, some clash of the rock, some despairing shouts from above—something had attracted the attention of the pilgrim laggards there. It was unlikely that those laggards could have made out much of what was happening on the hillside above them. Nevertheless, they sensed that it meant danger.

As a result, most of them were taking rapidly to their heels, racing up the path toward the defile well ahead. A few had redoubled their efforts around the ass. They pushed and tugged at the confused animal. He responded by kicking out vigorously with his hind legs. Some parts of his ample load had already come loose and more of it threatened to shift, and drag the poor beast physically into the ditch beside the path. The spectacle afforded Martin more time than he would otherwise have had. The bandits were divided in their response to it. Their intended victims were escaping. For practical purposes, some already had. Others surely would. Their lead was already too big. Perhaps only the pack animal and whatever of value he might be carrying was likely to be taken now.

Five of the bandits now abruptly broke from the cover of the pine grove and went sprinting down the incline towards the valley trail. At sight of them, the remaining pilgrims abandoned the struggle with the stubborn pack animal and fled after their fellows. Left to himself, the tired beast began to graze amidst the stubble at the side of the track.

Below Martin, the remaining brigands occupied themselves differently. The one with the injured shoulder simply sat down where he was safe from the possibility of more rocks from above, with his back against a large trunk. The one who had been stuck on the head still lay without moving. But the other three moved cautiously back toward the point where the ledge become a path, slanting down toward the more gentle slope of the hillside. They moved rapidly and with purpose. Their intent was clear. They had every determination to kill their erstwhile tormentor as quickly and as messily as possible.

Since all three had bows and carried arrows in hand, their quarry snatched up his bedroll and covered as much of his left side with it as he could. Then he began his retreat up the path, keeping as close to the rocky back edge of the hillside as the footing permitted. His pursuers could see him clearly now and set up a hunting shout. They might easily have loosed an arrow or two after him but they evidently disdained to waste a missile on him. For the moment they were moving away from him but they could already see the beginning of the path up to the ledge. In a moment or two, they would begin a really hot pursuit.

Martin knew from his explorations of the night before that he could not be trapped up here. The trail ran along, rounding a considerable outcrop of bare stone before it began a long, gradual descent of the hillside. Fortunately, his pursuers had not thought to send one of their number along the hillside to flank him. Still, he knew that once they too had reached that outcrop, he would be in easy sight, if not range, and there would be no cover of any kind until he reached the forest scrub well beyond the path's end.

The moment he lost sight of them as they discovered and began to ascend the path leading up to his ledge, he struck out at as fast a run as the uneven path permitted. His racing mind told him that he had every chance of being killed. He could not well elude them. The odds were three to one that one of his pursuers would be faster than he himself. If somehow their companions on the valley floor became aware of the grim game being played out above them, they would be in fair position to cut him off before he could reach any kind of cover. When those behind him came into a position at the head of the path's descent, they were sure to begin shooting in hope of a lucky strike. He himself, then, would have to slow a little if only to duck and veer to elude their aim.

Martin was past the outcrop of rock now and he began to pick up speed, aided by the ground's incline. He must not go too fast. Footing was more important. A turned ankle now would mean sure death. Unpleasant death. He was sweating profusely. For an instant, he stopped and slung the bedroll across his back, seeking whatever protection it might offer. He could still see the other bandits. So far, they were wrestling with the obdurate jackass which had been abused by a sufficient number of humans for one morning. The little beast lashed out with his hooves but there were too many of his captors. They struggled with the lashing of his pack, eager to examine their loot. If he was lucky, it would be of sufficient richness to distract them for a little time as yet.

He plunged on. A shaft rattled across the stones just alongside him. The other three robbers had reached the heights behind and had him in view. Now the footrace would begin in earnest.

Fortunately, the long months of trekking with the pilgrim band across the northern plain had burned off what little fat he might have accumulated about the old farm. His breath came in regular draughts and his legs gave him no real pain yet. The only urgency was for some promise of eventual concealment from the men behind him. He also needed a line of flight that would avoid his being cut off by the brigands in the valley, if they should see him. But there was none. They might catch sight of him at any moment now. Where the valley rose and narrowed ahead there were the usual stands of pine. But Martin was not sure that any of them grew thickly enough to permit him to elude pursuit. He doubted that he could outrun every one of the eight or nine who might give chase.

Another arrow struck in the ground, quivering, just ahead of him. Almost at the same time a shout went up off to his left, among the men clustered about the ass. He could see two of them break off and begin to run along the track which would converge with his own path up ahead.

He must sacrifice everything to more speed now. Dropping his bedroll, he bent forward and increased his tempo. No time now to glance behind. He veered slightly from moment to moment and made himself as small a target as he could but his life now depended above all on the best speed he could make.

At least he was not burdened by a weapon. The small knife in his belt was not a hindrance to his flight—but it would serve no real purpose if he were to be caught.

The fugitive dared not look behind for fear of tripping at this breakneck pace. He could see the two men on the valley track closing on him as their paths gradually drew together. At least they did not have bows. They must have put them aside in their struggles with the pack animal and must not have thought to retrieve them in their hasty decision to join the pursuit. But that would not matter much if they intercepted him.

Straining, he forced more speed from his protesting legs. When he, forced by the narrowing of the terrain, finally sped onto the main track itself, Martin was little more than a good spear cast in front of the nearest of them.

The track was climbing more abuptly now. With all his efforts, his speed must inevitably decrease somewhat. That meant that the bowmen behind him, still on relatively level, or even descending, ground would close the gap for a little time yet. They would have their best shots at him in a moment or two.

He was panting. Each gasp burned in his throat. His flight now carried him far enough forward that he could see the mouth of a ravine to his right. It would offer some cover from arrows. But unless it ran upwards, farther into the hills, it would be a death trap.

Another arrow whistled past. When it hit, well beyond him, it was clear that he was now in easy bow range. For the next few moments, simply running would not suffice. They could not miss forever. Having come almost parallel to it, Martin could now see that the ravine offered a dense mass of scrub in addition to a considerable stand of pine. He had to take the chance.

He lunged violently to the right. Behind him a shout of victory went up. They had run him to earth. Now they would dig him out and repay him, at some leisure, for all of the trouble he had given them.

Martin was not so sure. The time that he had for decision was short. Within the shelter of the pines the density of the scrub, vines, and bushes, increased sharply. It almost threatened to block his farther flight until he spied a narrow and low path, almost like a tunnel, in the underbrush. Something in the back of his mind moved uneasily at that sight but he had no choice. Behind him the bandits were at the mouth of the ravine.

He ducked lower and fled into the mouth of the cavity. Quickly, even the sunlight scarcely filtered in through the canopy above him. But here the ground itself was largely clear. Only his half-stoop hindered his speed along the pathway. The growth was deadening the sound of the pursuit. Or had they stopped?

That thought was, at first, so remarkable that the fugitive allowed himself a full pause. He heard nothing. Taking more time still, he strained, and strained again, to listen. But only the stirring of the breeze in the forest canopy above him was to be heard. Had they stopped?

Half-crouched there, Martin caught the scent. Suddenly, his mind screamed at him what it had sensed all along. This was a pig trail! There was no mistaking the rank, fetid odor. It hung from every bush. Now that he had eyes for something besides the pursuit behind him, the signs of rooting were evident everywhere.

Of course they had not followed him. They might wait for him to retreat into their hands but they would not enter such a tunnel. Even hunters with boar spears and dogs would not attempt it.

Martin suspected that there would be branching trails ahead. If this was the main trackway of the beast, his hope lay in reaching one of them. Somewhere in this maze was the creature's lair. His only hope was to discover a sidepath that led away from it, into the open, farther back in the ravine.

He had exchanged one kind of hunter for another. Every nerve now poised, eyes searching every slightest motion, ears anxiously alert to every vagrant sound, Martin crept quietly forward. From breakneck speed, he now was slowed to hardly more than a shuffle. Every step was taken gingerly, avoiding the scant debris that would give the least sound to a weight carelessly placed.

There must be, along here somewhere, a break in the undergrowth that would betray a companion trail. It might offer the wrong choice but his nerves shrieked for some alternative. This track was becoming dimmer, the farther he progressed along it. It was closing in upon him.

There it was! He had not heard it! Its bulk, in the half-light, was enormous. For all of that, he had not heard it! Now it stood before him on the trail, its height half of his own. The great head swung from side to side slowly, almost blocking the trail itself. And behind the slope of that head, Martin could see the massive shoulder hump where the terrible power of the brute was stored.

Its wicked little eyes were fixed on the intruder. The mouth hung open, under the snout, and thick beads of saliva dripped randomly to the floor of the path. The man could see the tusks, one of them broken off entirely, close to the root, but as thick and long as one of his own fingers. This close the smell of the beast was terrifying, almost overpowering of itself. The thing looked more like a devil than a simple animal.

How long will he take to make his kill, Martin wondered. It would eat him, surely. As a small boy he had seen the voracious appetites of hogs as they ate one of the farm's injured dogs. Nor had they bothered to kill it before they began to feed on it.

He thought of the knife in his belt. Could he get to it before the animal entirely disabled him? Could he open enough of a vein with it so that he would at least bleed to death rapidly?

Afterwards, who would he see? Images flashed through his mind. Claire? Therese? Ermentrude? All of them? What would they make of him? Or then, would he be likely to see any of them?

He could feel his strength draining away. He was unable to move. He was paralyzed in the face of the great beast.

Lord, forgive me. Forgive me my sins. Remember the little good that I have tried to do. Forgive my carelessness. Forgive my passion. Forgive my stupidity and my anger. Did my father die like this? I did not mean it.

Just that quickly, the monster was gone! It had twitched—then it had wheeled! Then, with an agility entirely belying its bulk, the brute had vanished into the underbrush at the side of the trail. There was no crashing. There was scarcely a movement of the weeds and saplings—but it was gone.

Martin was afraid to move. The great pig might reappear. It might come upon him from any direction in the midst of this scrub, which it knew and he did not.

He did not so much as breath. Then, the strength in his legs drained away. He fell. For a long time he knelt there in the dirt of the forest floor on all fours, in the posture of supplication.

Chapter Seventeen

When he came upon the pilgrims, two and a half days later, they were just stoking up the dinner fires. It was a pleasant place, here by the river, in the midst of the mountains. Firewood was plentiful for a change, even though it might be wet with the perpetual damp of the hills. The evening mists hung low over the valley already, and the heavy smoke of the campfires blended with it. Just then, in some emotional and hugely satisfying fashion, Martin felt himself home.

"Hey, look who's showed up!"

It was one of Rainald's guard. A big, French fellow who had survived the entire trip so far. There was then a general chorus of greeting, before the pilgrims went back to the business of preparing the evening meal.

In the midst of it, Father Simon came bustling, almost pushing through the throng. His short, plump body was agitated and his jaws and eyes worked furiously to contain the depth of his feelings. He threw his arms about Martin and pounded vigorously on his back with his fists.

"Martin, you've come back to us. Thank God for that! Are you all right?"

Martin had to smile broadly himself at the little priest's

welcome and his obvious affection. He realized now that he had intended this return all through the last few days. He was at home here—although he had not thought of it in just that way before now.

"Yes, yes, Simon. I am sound of body. It is good to see you. It is good to see all of you."

"Most touching."

The knight had come up and was observing the two from a few paces off. Now he walked completely around Martin, slowly surveying him from head to foot. Everyone else fell back and became silent.

"You seem to be somewhat the worse for wear, my dear Martin. You left us as my steward and you come back a fugitive—without boots, without gear of any kind from what I can see—and your tunic in rags and tatters.

"Well, we can repair most of that. Get yourself some food and then whatever you may need from the store cart. Don't be stingy about it. We've had more bedrolls and blankets than people for some weeks now. And you will have enough to do shortly. We break camp tomorrow for Santiago de Compostela."

So saying, Rainald walked off toward his own tent site.

"After you have tended to all those matters, come to see me later in the evening. I will have much in the way of instructions for you."

This last the knight called back over his shoulder as he moved away.

"Come Martin, share a meal with me," Simon said. "We can get to the rest later."

In his eagerness, the little priest was drawing him by the arm. The two proceeded to a small fire in the shelter of the lead cart that Simon ordinarily drove. A dark-looking stew of something, but what would be hard to say, bubbled in a pot slung on a tripod over the embers. There were rocks around the fire, close enough to have warmed, and the priest now removed a number of pieces of flatbread from a pouch and laid them across the stones to warm. Then he sat. Martin already had.

Reaching behind him, the cleric loosed a wineskin from the axletree of the cart on which it hung. He proferred it to his friend while looking at him closely, even anxiously. Martin accepted the skin with thanks, and took a substantial draught before returning it. Simon helped himself to a drink before returning the skin to its peg.

"What does one say to a man who has buried three wives?" The priest spoke with his eyes averted, stirring the contents of the cook pot with the point of his knife. His companion smiled at the obvious discomfort of his friend.

"I suppose a friend would advise him not to marry again." Now the little cleric looked up and smiled in turn. Martin had come beyond the first stages of his grief then. Carefully, he ventured further.

"You found a decent burial for Ermentrude then?"

"I found a Mass and then a grave for her just beyond the walls of León. There's a chapel of Saint Martin there and a French priest to serve it."

"That is more comfort than most of our number have had. You know, we must have buried—what?—more than thirty people since we left France. That's better than a third of those who started the pilgrimage with us."

He chose a piece of bread from the nearest rock and handed it to Martin. He took one for himself as well, and the two men began to ladle the stew into its folds. They ate busily for a time, until the little pot was almost empty. Then they dipped the remaining portions of bread into the broth, wiping the sides of the pot until the thin coating left began to burn black. Simon took the pot and tripod off the fire and again stretched the wineskin to his friend.

"You decided to rejoin us. Is there that much here for you now?"

"I took a vow of pilgrimage. That explains it, I suppose. I will say that I thought of other things. Even two days ago I was not sure what I would end by doing."

"There are other pilgrim bands along this road. You might have joined one of them. At least, there would have been no one there that hates you.

"You made a dangerous choice. Nothing has changed here. Rainald is as violent and touchy as ever. We've been here for some four days, repairing carts for the worst part of the journey. The happiest thing one can say is that the pilgrimage is about nine-tenths done."

"I don't think that Rainald hates me. He needs a victim and somehow I keep presenting myself as the most satisfying prey."

"Do you actually believe that he would have left us all here on our own and sought to find you if you hadn't returned?"

"Probably he would have done just that. It is the sort of challenge that appeals to his vanity. Whether or not he would have been able to find me is another matter. But I would not have run from him. I am too stubborn for that, my friend. It would have been like letting him beat me."

"No. We'll finish it together, you and I. We'll get to see what Compostela looks like and what the good saint has to offer us."

He rose now, and the men went together to the supply cart to see what Martin would need for the approaching night and the tomorrows to come. Later, after he'd found a satisfactory place to sleep, he sought out the knight.

"Well, always the faithful steward, eh Martin?"

"Just so, my lord, just so."

"Don't repeat yourself to me, Martin, it makes you sound impertinent. Did you find a suitable resting place for your late wife?"

"I buried her outside León, my lord, in a proper graveyard and after a proper requiem Mass. I could not do less."

"My God, you are such a 'proper' man. Was it this exaggerated sense of duty—of what is fitting—that brought you back to me? Or was it, rather, that you knew quite well that I would hunt you down if you didn't return?"

"I came back to finish the pilgrimage because I had taken a vow to do so. But I knew very well that, if I did not return, you would have tried to find me."

"Tried? Tried? Have you grown so great in your absence, Martin? What has changed you? Do you really think now that, if I chose to hunt you and kill you, that I would not succeed?"

"Be that as it may, my lord, I returned to this pilgrimage because it is my purpose to complete it."

There was ever a menace about the knight. It was even present when his mood was at its lightest. He never required the spur of temper for his cruelty. Good humor, or what in him passed for it, was no bar.

He now coolly surveyed the man before him. Rainald was no fool and his judgment of men was acute. Martin was taking a tack with him that was new. It was exciting. It was interesting. Real opposition, intelligent opposition, always challenged him.

"Sit down, Martin. Join me for a little wine. You must tell me of your adventures—for I believe that you must have had adventures. You have grown so!"

The other sat and half-reclined against a sack near the knight's tent. He was not sure what it was that he cared to say to the man. He had grown unused to the constant hectoring that had marked their relationship during the time up until

Ermentrude's death. Even so, he found that he did desire, quite deeply now, to complete the pilgrimage to Santiago de Compostela. Practically, that meant that he must tolerate the man's arrogance in some degree.

He must fashion some mixture of independence and service and amusement that would allow him to keep his own self-respect while it furnished such entertainment to Rainald as would move that volatile warrior to tolerate his steward's continuance in the band. For the moment, if the man wanted adventures, then adventures he would supply.

"I fear, my lord, that my poor life is not terribly exciting to one such as yourself, raised in the halls of the great and accustomed to the ways of violence."

"Come, come, Martin! False humility sits on you very badly—since you have no real humility. You are really quite satisfied with yourself, you know."

"Well, does a brush with suicide count as adventure? I considered it seriously after I buried Ermentrude."

"Suicide? How did you propose to do it?'

"I came very close simply to letting myself drown in the river just outside León."

"Suicide by drowning. That was a very rational choice for one such as yourself, Martin. You were a man far from home and with no intention of ever returning home. You were a man who had just buried a wife whom he had never even loved and about whom, therefore, he felt some considerable guilt. You were a man who faced sure death if he returned to his companions—and who was equally sure to be hunted down if he failed to return to them.

"Yes, I would say that suicide must have been definitely attractive and a perfectly reasonable road out of your difficulties. Why did you let such a marvelous chance slip?"

"I'm not sure. At one moment it just seemed like a good

thing to do and the next moment it didn't. The water was suddenly too cold and the sun too warm."

"Spoken like a true peasant! So what did you do then?"

"I came out of the water and found that somebody had stolen my boots."

Rainald looked at him in pure disbelief. Then the knight threw back his head and roared. For the first time since Martin had known him, he positively shook with merriment. For a considerable space of time he was unable to stop. He would pause, gasp for air, but then the total absurdity of the situation that the other had described would catch him again, sending him into new gales of laughter. Finally, with difficulty, he regained control.

"Oh Martin, just when I have hopes that you are about to do something serious with your life, you let some oaf steal your boots. I really should not let you wander about the countryside by yourself. Someone will steal your tunic next, while you are asleep, and you will be left as naked in body as you are in mind.

"And suicide would have been such a dignified choice. I, myself, have often thought that there are many embarassments in life to which I would unhesitatingly choose suicide rather than endure.

"And drowning is such a good method for it, don't you think? Dignified, serene even. A certain style about it. I have thought sometimes, during this trip, that I might decide finally to simply ride Alexander out into the western sea until we both sank beneath the waves forever. I would do it in full armor, of course, and attired like a gentleman. But then, it would have to be for a serious reason.

"But you, you—likely someone would steal your horse."

The knight chuckled again. Then he sobered and proffered the wineskin to his steward.

"Have you had adventures of a more serious nature? Surely, even you must have your serious moments."

Martin refreshed himself with the skin. For the first time ever in their conversations he felt that he was toying with the knight, rather than the other way about. If he persisted, Rainald would realize it soon enough. Still, what did that matter? So long as he did not provoke the other into outright murderous violence. He had no particular desire to die just yet. The man was not his friend—would never be his friend. If the hostility between them bubbled to the surface, let it.

"I made another attempt at suicide later."

"You needed practice? Obviously you still do. But such reiteration can get boring. What went wrong this other time?"

And so Martin recounted the story of his attack on the bandits in the valley amidst the mountains of León. The knight listened—fascinated despite himself.

"Why would you do such a thing? No weapon but a handful of rocks. The odds were ten to one, you say? This is a challenge worthy of Hercules himself! Did you actually have suicide, a heroic death, in mind?"

"No. By this time I had well decided that I wanted to live. But the low cunning of the outlaws and the stupidity and vulnerability of the pilgrims below just made me angry. I just did not want them to succeed. If I had had some real weapons I might have tried to kill them all."

"The David of the Lord smiting the Philistines, eh? By God, Martin, you are making yourself responsible for the reign of justice on earth. No wonder that you have become such a dangerous man. Sooner or later you will indeed find yourself a bloody death—probably sooner. But that filthy bunch must have turned on you. How did you escape?"

"I ran."

"Of course. But it is a lucky man who can outrun six or seven pursuers."

"Yes. They would have caught me. But I happened to find a wild pig's run and fled into that. They didn't follow me."

"I'd warrant that they did not. Who would? Encountering the boar on his own turf is a chance that no one but an idiot or a suicide would risk. You're lucky that you did not meet one."

"But I did."

Rainald looked at him closely. The man was serious.

"What happened?"

"Nothing. The black devil just stared at me. He seemed the size of a horse—of your Alexander—in that little run. My feet were fixed to the ground. There was no where to go. I tried to imagine what sort of death I was about to meet.

"Then the beast vanished into thin air. I'm not sure that I even blinked. I couldn't have taken my eyes off him. I was too terrified for that. But suddenly he was gone. The brute must have turned off into the brush but I never saw him do it, nor heard his crashing off, nor did I so much as see a leaf tremble at his passing. And I myself have been a hunter of wild animals."

Martin found himself sweating at the recounting of his escape. The knight regarded him with some puzzlement. After a moment, he spoke.

"In your own way, Martin, I fear that you are a religious man. Did you perhaps, in your agitation, make the sign of the cross. Perhaps it was not a boar at all but rather a fiend of some kind that you met. I have never heard of a boar giving ground to one puny man. Beside that, as big as they are, they leave a trail in heavy brush that the dullest tracker can detect."

"If it was a devil, it was a very solid one, my lord. I could hear his breathing and the stink of him was almost enough to choke me. But after he disappeared, I was so startled that, in truth, I cannot remember whether or not his stench hung in the air after him."

Rainald stirred, then got up. He paced a bit, restlessly. Finally, he returned to his seat. Full night, by this time, surrounded them.

"You tell a strange tale, my friend. But then, we have had a strange journey together, you and I, strange from its beginning. It must come to an end quickly. That is evident enough. Otherwise, we should come into Santiago de Compostela together and I have assured you many times that this will not happen.

"Why is it that it has come to matter to me? I have killed men like yourself many a time. But they didn't hang on. They didn't attach themselves to me. They didn't seek their own death—and grow in character before my very eyes because of such a seeking. Or, if they did, they did not interest me enough for it to attract my notice."

Martin thought that there was no answer to this sort of musing. In any event, the knight likely did not wish one. He sat and waited. Meanwhile, Rainald became visibly more agitated.

"What is it that you want, Martin?

"To finish the pilgrimage, my lord."

"But that you will not do. The only possible way in which you could achieve that would be to become in reality my steward. You grudgingly accept that position for now. But if we should reach Compostela, you would desert me in a moment.

"This I find intolerable. You, whom I found a peasant deserted on the trail. You, whom I have turned into a good ostler, into something of a soldier, into a passable trail boss, you set yourself up in judgment over me! My service is not good enough for you. In every way but words, you call yourself my better. It will not do, Martin, it will not do!"

The man is close to madness, Martin thought. He studied the fire which had burned almost to embers, avoiding the knight's gaze. In the long silence, their crack and snap echoed louder and louder.

"By God, you are a stubborn brute. To save your very life, you will not yield to me. I could teach you much. Together we could make a name, here in this forsaken land of miserable horses and brutish men. Remember that popinjay king, Alfonso? He offered to take me into his service when this pilgrimage was complete. You would wonder at what I would accomplish. You could share in that."

The words hung in the air. Again Martin made no answer.

"Very well! You will live this night. I give you that. But I will come for you. Mark me! Wonder when it will be, Martin, wonder when it will be! See if your guts don't shrivel just a little in the waiting. You will not die pleasantly. I assure you of that.

"For now, get to your bed. You will work for me so long as I require it—but it will not save you now."

Chapter Eighteen

For three days the band had been toiling upward into the mountains. The old discipline of the trail had reasserted itself quickly enough but the terrain was different. The entire surroundings were different. The mountains that they had crossed from France had been higher, certainly. But that passage had been relatively quick. These peaks promised to go on forever, to run down into the western sea itself, perhaps. More, for two months they had been suffering from the unrelenting heat of the great plain that they had traversed. Their bodies had boiled and their skin had cracked with the constant sun and the near absence of water.

Now they were cold—cold with the damp mist that began when the sun had not yet set but merely dropped beyond the crest immediately before them. From that moment, moisture reigned. Creeping under the clothes, chilling the body, it was master of life until long after the journey had resumed the following morning. Blankets were wet. Food mildewed. Brushwood was impossible to come by dry enough to make a fire free enough from smoke, so that a man could sit within a half-dozen lengths of it and warm himself through.

On the great plain, one had been able to see to the horizon itself. Danger forecast its approach long in advance. But mostly, the plains had been empty. Here the brush pushed down to the very edges of the carts themselves. One could not see half a spear's cast, so thick was the underbrush. In the rear of the column, a man could hear the vanguard crashing and cursing along but, most usually, it was impossible to see it.

This country teemed with animals that might delight the knight—God blight him—and small meats of hare and such were both newly common and welcome. Still, the night air rang with the howl of wolves and one man, going to relieve himself at some little distance out from the camp, had been set upon and seriously mauled by a bear. He lay now in the bed of the third of the carts, moaning and feverish. He probably would be dead soon. On the second day, shortly after they had broken camp, a great black boar had broken out of the morning mists, crashed through the middle of the line of march, and vanished without a trace into the brush and mist of its farther side.

And then there were the carts. They caught on everything in this close environment. They had to be maneuvered around outcrops where the path narrowed and the ground fell away. A man must take care that he was neither trapped between their side and the cliff face nor nudged into the abyss below as they slid about. They had to be lifted often over great rocks embedded in the trail, on which their clumsy wheels hung up. The oxen had to be stopped soon enough then. Otherwise the stupid beasts might pull the cart apart if the rocks refused to give way given the unrelenting tug of those great shoulders.

Already two carts had been abandoned—their loads transferred into the remaining four. What was needed here were pack animals. In the valley behind, such animals were to be had but the asking prices had seemed steep then. They didn't now. For one reason or another, Rainald had chosen not to purchase any. Now, one cursed and heaved and sweated in the mist. At the same time, you tried to be careful and not to have a wheel roll over your foot. Martin, was everywhere—working as hard as any man—but asses' backs were needed, not men's. Rainald kept his own beasts to himself. The humble ones were loaded with his own gear solely and the great ones were too grand—like their master—to do common work.

Martin knew these feelings. How could he not? They were the inevitable stuff out of every mouth that had breath enough to voice anything at all. He reminded them of how far they had come. He pointed out that their journey, their pilgrimage, was now within mere weeks, not months, of its completion. Sullenly, they refused to dispute him. They coughed and shivered and quarreled with one another for little or no reason. Cart-length by painful cart-length the band ground ahead.

Rainald was quite as aware of the pilgrims' feelings as was his steward. He regarded it with scarcely concealed amusement. The more problems it created for his steward, the more it served his own purposes. The man should sweat and worry! His arrogant back should break! His own kind—his precious louts and commoners—were very fit to be his trial, his undoing. In the meantime though, he was holding them together. He was moving them along despite all difficulties. Very good. In that process, he was keeping himself alive. He was making himself indispensable—for the time being. Nonetheless, the knight could detect no anxiety in the man. He worked without visible trace of concern for his own life. Well, give it time—there was some left yet. The man needed to feel terror before the moment for his dispatch could arrive.

Yet once more the day had come in rain and mist. Martin was standing, taking a moment of respite, next to Simon. The little priest, still driving the lead cart, had most of the responsibility for deciding where it, and its fellows, could pass and where they could not. It was he who called the halt and asked for men to heave at the stones in their path. He was the one who called back down the line for axmen, or for men with ropes, or just simply for strong backs to muscle the carts forward. Consequently, the priest was the one who was most cursed by the rest of the column—at least, after the knight himself. It was ironic as his decisions were mostly sound and—in the end—saved labor. Nevertheless, he was the taskmaster of the first instance and was, inevitably, roundly abused for that very fact.

"The sun may out by midday if we're lucky, Simon," Martin observed.

"The Lord makes his sun to shine upon sinner and saint alike, then."

"Come now, Father, do you really think that there can be even a single saint in this column? Your God is more generous than you credit."

"You are probably right, my friend. Every day, as wheels crack, provisions spill, and limbs split, I wonder what game it is that Providence plays with us. Whether there is a Divine Providence at all. Then, at night, in my blanketroll, I think back over the months of this journey and am amazed that any of us have survived to come so far. That thought quite revives my faith. Not that I scant your own efforts, not at all."

"You are a rock, Simon, truly a rock."

"Let's not start the day with a blasphemy, Martin. There will be disasters enough before we see your midday sun."

"Your night's bed must have been wet, indeed, my small friend, if you begin the day full of such ominous ruminations. I'll see if I can find you better for the coming night. Right now, better whip up the oxen. We need to get under way before our knight friend comes cantering grandly back to urge us forward with kind words."

Simon climbed stiffly into his cart, untied the reins from the end post, and laid his whip smartly across the flanks of the team. Roused from sleep, or what looked very like it, the great beasts shuffled, snorted quietly, and tried a tentative thrust against the yoke. Twigs snapped, the cart groaned and creaked, and the massive wheels turned a full revolution. The day had officially begun.

Behind the small priest, Martin began to shout the remainder of the column into motion. The other three carts fell into a ragged line behind Simon's. After some hesitation, the forty-odd remaining pilgrims stumbled and pushed their way into a line of march. Some of them had still to finish rolling their beds, and they confused and bothered everyone with their attempts to do so while actually walking. It was a typical morning.

The steward watched them pass, encouraging some, shouting abuse at others—but the latter not seriously. It was far too early in the day for real threats. Save them for later.

The three asses that still survived were hustled forward by their ostlers. They were seriously overloaded; Martin could see that. Still, none of the beasts appeared to be limping, much less lame. By tomorrow, they would be a little less burdened. Some of the stuff of their packs would be lost today, some of it would be thrown away, and still other portions of it would be eaten.

No need to hustle forward that lot. They spent a good part of their time looking back over their shoulders as it was. Behind them came Rainald's stallions. Each had one of his men-at-arms serving him as groom. The men were more or less used to their charges by now and were alert to the capacity for troublemaking in the volatile Julius and, to a lesser degree, in Alexander. But, whenever one of them relaxed their watchfulness for very long, the ostlers ahead, or their animals, were likely to be favored with a bite or a shoulder that pitched them toward the brush at the side of the path.

Martin squinted closely at the great horses. They'd been groomed adequately. There was no sign of sores or irregularity in their gaits. Their tails were clean and their breath came clear and full. Soon now, the knight would ride back to see that his darlings were well. God forbid that they should not be.

The last of the three men-at-arms followed the stallions. They were not too close. The animals' hooves had taught respect early on in this station. Their presence at the column's rear assured that no enterprising hill bandit would easily run off with any of the pack animals. Martin fell in with them. He wanted to inquire more closely about the condition of the stallions. Anyway, he enjoyed their company usually. Most of the time they had little to do except to watch that their feet did not stray into the morning dung that the animals just ahead of them produced in fair quantities.

Only when the most serious obstacles to the band's progress developed were these men summoned to lend a shoulder or a back. Two more of their fellow men-at-arms marched with the knight at the tip of the column. Martin rotated their stations regularly, in the interests of fairness, though it would be difficult to say which of the posts was easier. Still, men-at-arms would find quick cause for complaint, any complaint, if he did not do so.

Martin still marched with them when Rainald appeared, emerging from the heavier-than-average ground fog. Ignoring the men, he swung his palfrey about, approaching Julius first, and then Alexander. The grooms leading them had to step smartly to avoid his mount. The knight spoke only to the stallions, leaning somewhat to stroke their necks and heads. Then he reined back. Apparently, he was satisfied with what he saw. One knew quickly enough when he wasn't. He moved off at a half-trot and those ahead experienced with his ways, rapidly scattered at his approach.

Martin watched him go. They no longer spoke except by way of command or his own answer to a command or question. That made life simpler for him. It may also make it shorter, he reflected ruefully. Well, the column must be in order for now. Likely, before long, it wouldn't be. It wasn't moving very fast but he had come not to expect that.

He was still with the rearguard, some little time later, when he heard the first shouts up ahead. In a moment, he was at a run. Those immediately before him were still in motion, although fearfully. Past them, the walkers had ground to a halt. The trouble was just beyond them.

The last cart was slewed halfway about in the path. The right ox of its team presented its flank to him. There must have been five, maybe six arrows, protruding from its gut and flanks. Its head tossed and its eye rolled. The beast lowed in pain, and pulled his mate across the path with him.

Martin had already uncased his bow and now he strung it. He dropped to one knee and scanned the wall of brush stretching above the animals. In front of them, the other carts had now stopped at some distance. Whoever possessed a weapon scrambled to find it. Men ducked behind carts or pressed as close as they could get to the low bank from which the scrub forest rose.

There was no sound but the plaintive lowing of the dying ox and the panicky grunting of his yoke mate. No screaming yet. No more arrows yet. No war cries from the trees. The silence grew.

To his left, Martin became conscious of the approach of the knight. The man picked his way though the growing tangle of carts and men. He had donned his helm and his sword was drawn.

He looked ready to urge his palfrey up into the treeline, but so far, could find no target to be ridden down. To keep his mount from becoming an easy target, he maneuvered his horse back and forth in what room the path allowed. The chink of his weapons could just be heard above the groans of the ox.

Still, there were no more arrows. The silence was unbroken. No one wished to call the attention of the unseen bowmen to himself. Then, remarkably, one of the men-at-arms from the rearguard appeared among the trees above. He was waving vigorously. His two mates joined him almost at once. Martin unnocked his arrow and so did most of the others. Louis, the leader among them, half-slid, half-stumbled down to the path.

"There must have been three or seven or eight of them up there. The brush is that trampled down. One of them took a crap about five hours ago. They were waiting for us, for sure. But they are long gone now."

Rainald was only half-listening. He had dismounted and was examining the ox. It had bled profusely and was now near dead. By main force he wrenched one of the arrows out of its side. There was a further gush of blood but the animal hardly twitched.

"Look at this. Poor stuff."

He held the arrow out for the inspection of the man-at-arms. The man gave it a perfunctory glance.

"Home made. Bad shaft. Bad feathers. No armorer ever turned that one out. Local bandits. But what were they trying to do? They aren't well enough armed or numerous enough to have taken us on—even with the advantage of surprise. Why bother if you are only going to kill one lousy ox."

"The bastards did exactly what they intended. They're hungry. They killed the ox for the same reason that anyone does. They wanted him to eat."

The knight turned to Martin.

"Get the other ox out of that yoke. Lead him off and tether him with the pack animals. We may have need of him later. Off-load the cart and distribute that stuff wherever it will ride best. Then I want the dead one butchered. The heart and the liver, the haunches and loins can go into the third cart. Puncture the gall sac and let it drain all over the rest of the entrails."

It took a good half hour to carry out his instructions. Meanwhile the men-at-arms continued to search the brush above the trail but they found nothing but a cold trail. Finally the bloody business was finished.

"Now load what's left into the cart and push the cart up here where the fall-off is steepest."

At Rainald's urging, the men moved swiftly.

"Now run the cart down off the path. Get it going with as much speed as you can."

There was a concerted heave and the wheels of the clumsy vehicle cleared the edge of the path. It moved slowly at first, appearing to be about to hang up on some fairly dense underbrush. Then its bulk began to tell and the cart picked up speed. On it ran, until it was well beyond a spear cast. Then a wheel caught on a substantial sapling and the whole cart slewed about and turned over completely before disappearing into some further brush.

Rainald surveyed the band, standing about, watching him.

"If the bastards can find what's left of the beast before the animals do, then they can have their meat. But we've at least made it difficult for them. They'll have reason to know that there is one pilgrim band that can't be pillaged at will.

"Now form up again and resume march. Keep a sharp eye but I doubt that they will bother us again today. They will be too busy trying to retrieve what meat they can. May the foul sons of bitches all starve!"

With the delay, the morning had so far advanced that the

sun had topped the high ridge before them and the mist rapidly began to disappear, lifting everyone's spirits. Not much after noon, the column reached the top of the ridge. From there they could see well into the distance, for subsequent hills seemed to gradually diminish in size, although their extent still reached to the horizon. No one could see an immediate end to the journey from there but the sense of it was palpable. For now, below them lay a small river valley bordered by substantial meadowlands. It promised a good camp for this night and the prospect of the lightening of their journey in the days to come. Everyone picked up their speed.

The night had been dark, very dark. But water had been plentiful and previous pilgrims had so beaten down the camping area that firepits were everywhere. The nearby woods were full of latrines and even more casual deposits of human and animal waste, so that some care was necessary. Martin had just decided, reluctantly, to get up and make use of them when the screaming began.

His sleep-fuddled brain took a little time to sort out what he was hearing. Finally, he realized no human throat was making such a sound. Oh Christ, it was the horses!

Immediately he was on his feet—running. Nevertheless, by the time he reached them Rainald was already there. Julius was down—his throat a great bloody gash. The stallion feebly thrashed its front legs. Its death throes were already beginning. Nearby, Alexander struggled in his hobble, anxious to escape the scene and the stink, neighing and plunging. Out of long instinct, Martin moved to control the great animal—first covering his eyes, then loosing the hobble, and finally leading the blinded animal away and surrendering him to the soldier, Louis, who had come up.

By the time he had completed these actions, Julius was dead. The knight stood over that stallion cursing quietly and without stop. Someone had brought up a flaming bough and, after a moment, Martin realized with a shock that tears coursed down the man's cheeks. It was the only outward sign of serious emotion that he had ever seen Rainald display.

"Louis, get my saddle on Alexander. Martin, get another on my pack animal and find your bow. You're coming with me."

Then he was gone, only to return carrying his heavy spear and girt with a sword. He had slipped a short coat of mail over his tunic and his helmet dangled from one hand by its chinstrap. He was snapping further orders to Louis when Martin came up with his bow and his mount.

"You're in charge while we're gone, man. I want Julius buried, and buried deep. No one will make a meal of him. After that, get the pilgrims ready to travel. Keep an eye out for more trouble but I don't think there will be more. They have already taken their revenge for yesterday.

"Martin and I should not be gone for more than two hours. The lot of them will be heading for cover in that marsh about three miles north of here—the one the scouts located yesterday after we made camp. The scum will be looking to hide there and laugh at us. But we can catch them before they make it there. They can't have but a few moment's lead on us. When we catch them, I'll separate every limb from their filthy bodies before they're lucky enough to be dead!"

Then he turned to his steward with a quick glance.

"Good. Fortunately for you, my friend, you're the best shot with a warbow I have. I'll have plenty of use for you this morning."

The knight started off, leading Alexander by the reins. He had located what he was fairly sure was the track of the marauders while Martin had been assembling his gear. Now he speeded up to a half-trot. Martin followed behind, mounted on the mule and straining to pierce the dark which had not yet softened to the half-light of dawning.

By the time that it had, the steward was marveling at the noble's ability to track a quarry under such circumstances. The men in front of them were making some attempt to throw off pursuit. They were keeping just inside of the forest's verge, but with some deeper penetration of its gloom from time to time and some doubling when they did so. Nonetheless, the general direction that they steadily maintained was toward the river marshes, as the knight had guessed from the outset.

The light had not been long with them, when Martin himself could begin to make out their trail. Possibly they had begun to relax their care. Or, on the other hand, they may have detected some sign of pursuit and were gambling everything on a dash for the protection of the marsh. It was, Martin estimated, only about a mile off. From the breadth of their track, he guessed that they numbered about a dozen.

Rainald swung up on Alexander finally. In the growing light, he could follow the track from horseback.

"Look to your bow, Martin. The bastards will be in sight soon enough. I want them for myself—all of them, if I can. But keep them off my back if you have to. Hang back.

"I don't see any sign that they have divided up and left a few to take us from behind. Probably they lack the courage for such tactics. Or maybe no one of them has the authority to order the others. It looks as though they are all running for cover as fast as they can. But hang back anyway. Make sure that no one gets behind you and surprises us."

With that, he swung the big horse and touched him ever so lightly with the spur. From long practice, the stallion's head went low and he began to lope forward. Rainald leaned across his neck, spear held loosely in his right hand. The two plunged through the trees and scrub with surprising speed and agility. Martin waited for a long moment, and then urged his mule on their track at a fast walk. There was no danger of losing them. It was more important to watch the trail and the bordering scrub.

"Saint Denis! Saint Denis!"

The battlecry of the knight sounded from in front. Rainald must have brought his prey into view. Martin kicked his own mount into a clumsy gallop. He arrived just in time to see it all.

The bandits had broken the forest cover to make more speed. Not far ahead of them its edge ran down to the very borders of the marsh. As far as one could see, back into bracken water and mud, the place teemed with sedge and cattails, all over-hung now with the early morning fog. Rainald could never pursue them into that refuge on Alexander. Doubtless they had knowledge of its trails and shallows. But the quarry was too far from its border. The big horse galloped with a speed that belied his bulk. He would eat up the distance that remained between them.

"Saint Denis! Saint Denis!"

Then suddenly the stallion was down! A rabbit's hole? A fox den? Martin—far back as he was—heard the snap of bone. The big horse's body twisted around his left leg as though it were a willow wand. His speed lifted Alexander's haunches from the ground and the whole of his body flew forward and sideways about that pivot.

There was no avoiding the suddenness of that fall and im-pact. Rainald's own left leg was crushed beneath his mount. Slowly, the knight strained forward. When he could just barely reach it, he stroked the neck of the stallion. The horse had be-gun to scream in pain. The man looked in vain for either his spear or his sword. Both had skidded out of reach. Instinc-tively, while falling, he had cast the spear well free of himself and his mount. When they hit, the force of that crash somehow had snapped his swordbelt and that weapon now lay just beyond Alexander's head, unreachable.

The thrashing of the great animal ground his leg against the dirt and sent waves of pain up into his stomach and chest. If that motion did not stop soon, it would kill him for sure. Worse than that, he might himself begin to scream—like the horse. Then, he heard the arrows thud into it and the sounds of the animal's agony died away into a deep gurgle and then ceased entirely.

From in front of the fallen warrior came shouts of excitement and triumph. The bandits had heard the crash of the stallion and a glance quickly revealed the hopeless position of their former pursuer.

Most probably, his very first exertions revealed to Rainald the impossibility of getting himself out from under the dead Alexander. Even if he could, his left leg was so badly smashed and broken that he could not crawl on it—much less stand.

To Martin's amazement, Rainald now began to draw the fringes of his short mail shirt from under his mount and to work it up across his chest. When he had done so, his gaze turned in search of Martin. Even over that distance, the steward could read the plea in the knight's eyes. Their gazes locked. Martin saw the familiar, ironic smile spread over the other's visage.

He drew the bowstring full to his ear and then released it. The broad-headed arrow struck Rainald in the right chest and threw him violently back, as far as his pinned leg permitted.

Before that motion was well over, another arrow followed hard upon, smashing through the ribs, and entering the lung cavity. The knight's left hand raised in the faintest of salutes and the tension drained from his face. Suddenly, blood poured from his lips and his head dropped forward.

Martin turned his mule and spurred it until the creature's flanks ran blood.

Chapter Nineteen

When they came down out of the hills that day into the object of their months-long journey, they found a town hardly larger than a score they had hurried past. What marked Santiago de Compostela as different was not its size or its wealth but the presence of a body of temporary inhabitants equal, or more than equal, to its regular population camped before its gates. They joined that mass of bodies, finding of course that it was never made up of the same persons for two days in a row. They were absorbed in its life and its rhythms easily and immediately.

On its outskirts they were hailed by traders and merchants who anticipated their need for food and clothing. Every arriving pilgrim brought much the same wants. To satisfy them, the major goods of the band were sold off. Carts were sold for what price those battered vehicles might command. The exhausted bullocks that had drawn them were sold for meat. Martin suspected that the entire routine of a quick sale on arrival benefited no one so much as the merchants who made a daily living at it, but the pressure on the pilgrims was irresistable. They would have their proceeds there and then. By common consent he was selected their spokesman and he yielded to their importunity.

His companions of the trail were particularly anxious that the pilgrimage be liquidated because the goods of Rainald represented a major windfall that might be lost if not disposed of rapidly. The palfrey, Dido, was the largest asset and the most conspicuous. In addition to the horse, there remained a fair number of the knight's weapons, a body-length mail tunic, a store of rich clothing, and the noble's campaign tent. Three of the merchants hastily pooled their resources to offer a better price than they might have otherwise for all of these. No less than the pilgrims themselves, the tradesmen wished to remove such remarkable goods from the possible attentions and certain avarice of local justices.

A bargain was struck. The goods of Rainald disappeared into the outskirts of the town with such swiftness as to suggest that they had never existed at all. Finally, all proceeds were shared out equally. As a result, the survivors of the journey had, at least initially, rather more in the way of assets to squander than most arriving pilgrims. If tender consciences in fact existed, they were easily salved at the thought of the injuries and indignities they had suffered at the knight's hands.

With the conclusion of that business, the pilgrimage band ceased to exist. Friendship and mutual dependence kept some of its individuals together until such time as they should decide to pursue a new life here at the end of the earth or take up their return journey. If the latter, they would find themselves a newly constituted group. Such bands formed daily. In the interim, they each became part of the pilgrim life that circulated through the town and its shrines.

At the center of these was the cathedral church of Saint

James. Although the old church was being partially dismantled, and the foundations of a grand, new church encircled the older fabric, yet that shrine had been the aim of their journey from the first and remained so. To reach its crypt and the mysterious marble cask that contained the relics of the great Saint James himself, they swarmed past masons and over half-laid courses of stone and fill. They fought past vendors of relics, vendors of trinkets, vendors of water, of sweets, and of other goods only just suggested, finally to trod the stairs down into the crypt, to jostle and kneel to pray, and at last to yield place to others pressing in behind them. When they emerged once more above ground, there still remained the dozen humbler churches and monasteries of the town in which to satisfy more leisurely devotions.

These were individual pursuits individually pursued. If they were part of the throng of faithful so engaged, they were no longer part of that particular pilgrim band that had so long trudged in common across the Iberian plain to reach this holy place. A few of them still knew where the priest, Simon, could be found—if anyone cared. No one could have told you what had become of Martin.

But this particular night, the smoke of a thousand charcoal fires filled his nose. Their soft, lazy glow was everywhere in the mammoth campground before the cathedral, promising warmth, promising food, outlining the seated and squatting figures of the immense throng of pilgrims. Lean-tos, bedrolls, even proper tents, formed constant obstacles to walking. Martin considered that if it came to that, he could be a charcoal vender. There was no shortage of customers.

This is stupid he thought. Either I should have gotten here while it was still light or I should simply have waited until morning. I'll never find him in this mass of people. Half of them don't even speak a language that I can understand. Those

I can understand all seem to be as confused as I am. In this dark they might as well be in the forest for all the sense of direction they have.

Everyone could identify the cathedral itself by its bulk, looming against the night sky, and the periodic sounding of its bells. Those were hung in a temporary shed, for the old bell towers had been torn down to make way for the new construction. The old church was back behind it, shorn of its one-time facade and waiting for a newer, grander one.

"Sorry. I didn't see you."

People sleeping on the ground without a fire or a tent were simply objects that you stepped on first—and around afterwards. It might improve if the moon would come up. Great, scudding mountains of inky clouds obliterated, and then revealed once more, the stars of the fall night in their passage. They hadn't rained on him today, since early morning, but the raw edge of the wind suggested that they might before long now.

Simon had said that he would try to get a spot near the stream that ran along the far edge of the pilgrims' campground. So, with his back to the old church, Martin thought he should be approaching it pretty soon now. He was listening for the sound of running water, water over rocks or the like. But the chorus of voices, none of them very loud in the dark, but hundreds of them at any given moment, murmuring, rasping, coughing, humming, filled his ears as wax might. Any individual sound was faint, muffled.

Actually, he almost walked into the water before he saw it. Not much of a stream. In the moonless night its surface reflected nothing but the lights of nearby campfires, giving the illusion of still further encampments to the unwary. So now, all he had to do was to pick a direction, right or left, and walk along the stream, asking as he went for news of the little French priest. He chose what seemed to be the longer portion of the stream's bed and followed it. And eventually, he did stumble over the cleric.

"You've come back, Martin. I had begun to doubt that you would. Have you fulfilled your pilgrim vow yet?"

"Not yet, Simon, not yet. I suppose that you have, my friend?"

"Yes. The first morning I awoke here I had myself confessed, I heard Mass in the cathedral, and I prayed before the sacred relics. Why would a man wait—after all that walking to get here?

"But you disappeared almost at once. You were gone already that first morning before I was up. Where have you been?"

"I walked out to see the ocean. It is not so far, you know. It's only a two day's walk from here."

"You walked out to see the ocean? After walking across half the world, you decided to walk yet farther? What was it like, this ocean?"

"Monstrous, my friend. It is huge. I had never seen the ocean before. Those great grey waters pound in as if to swallow up the land entirely. Its motion never stops. There is just that continual roar—and over it, only the crying of seabirds. Like lost souls. A man could be lost forever in its immensity. Even if one dies in the deep forest, the animals leave something—some bones, hair, a few teeth. That sea would leave nothing. It was terrifying. I decided to come back."

This was the moment that the tardy moon chose to make its appearance. The clouds broke and it was full, bathing the campground with its thin light. Simon regarded his friend carefully. He appeared the same. Nevertheless, something about the man had changed.

"Sit down, man, sit down. Will you have some food? I have some olives and some cheese. You are welcome to it. Perhaps a little wine? It is a chill night."

Martin merely shook his head.

"Where are the others?"

"Oh, they're here, camped about in the dark, sleeping or pursuing some less harmless activity. At least, those that haven't already departed are here. Some were quick to join other pilgrim bands ready to return, strange as that must seem. I think that they must have regretted their decision to come long, long before we arrived here and now they can't get home quickly enough.

"Others will never go home at all. One or two have already gotten married to local women. They'll find some business hereabouts—or some thievery, I dare say. Rainald's men-at-arms hired themselves out almost immediately. The world always has need of soldiers.

"In any event, our pilgrimage is over. Those who remain, no more than twenty by today and likely fewer tomorrow, could never make the journey back in safety. They'll have to join with some larger group. Everyone is doing that. One group or another leaves every day.

"And you? What about you, Martin, old friend?"

There was a pause. Martin was looking into the coals of Simon's small fire. In a bit, he looked up.

"I would like you to confess me, Simon. I've decided to complete my vow in the morning and so—I would like you to confess me this night."

"If you wish it, Martin, if you wish it. But it might be easier for you with some priest who doesn't know you. There are enough about."

"No. It will be simpler, I think, to confess to you, my friend. You already know a good part of it anyway. There will be less to explain."

The two men sat in silence for a time. Then, the moon disappeared once more, obscured by a cloud that promised to be long in passing.

"You know, Father, that I bear heavy responsibility for the death of my first wife, Claire. You can judge how much. I was young. I was in love—we both were. But even then I myself sometimes felt that my demands on her were unreasonable. Not that it made any difference in my actions. She never complained—not even when she was in her monthly flow. Even when she came with child, I pursued her, right up until the time when she became sick, her sixth month. I would not leave her rest. It may be that I was the reason why she became sick. I cared for her from then until she died—as best I could—but it was too late."

"You cannot know the extent of your fault here, Martin. Your story is not an uncommon one with young men, you know. It is enough that you repent and confess your failings. Leave the measurements to God."

"It seemed to me then that Claire's death was God's sentence on me. But that was terrible for her too, wasn't it? She was an innocent. She didn't do anything that a wife is not supposed to do. He let me kill her. It was my fault—but He let me do it.

"That is how I felt when I started with Therese. Oh, I loved her well enough. I lusted after her too. I needed her to fill the blackness in my life, in my soul. All those feelings were there. But there was more. In some way or other, she was my revenge on God. I enjoyed her all the more because He had taken my first love away from me. Every time I sated myself on her body, it was a celebration of His defeat too. I gloried in the touch and smell of her soft flesh.

"Understand me. I did not think these things so clearly then. I must have hidden at least a part of them from myself as well. I have only come to know what I really was doing over these past months on the way to Compostela.

"In those months, I believe that God led me on. He abandoned me to my own self. He looked away while my anger and my revenge led me to desert my own father. He knew all along that I would never go after the old man and bring him back home, once he had left. He knew that I was relieved to have the old man gone. It may be that I felt that my father understood too well what I was doing. It was awkward to have a witness to my quarrel with God.

"Then, He beat me again. He took Therese as well. Perhaps she wasn't a perfect woman. She used her body to trap me. But I knew that from the first. I connived at it. She was hardly more than a child. But she was a hungry child with no future. She committed no sin against me. God saw that she gave me a full measure of herself. Except in my heart, it was an honest bargain. She kept it, even to the carrying of my child. Therese never suspected that she was part of my stubborn determination to revenge myself on God.

"So when God took Therese—killed Therese I said then—I gave the fight up. I didn't forgive Him, but I stopped fighting Him. I gave it all up, everything: the farm, the house, the land, my life. I took up the pilgrim's staff and left."

Martin's voice trailed off. He stared into the coals. The moonlight played on his impassive features. Simon waited for a bit to see whether or not he wanted to resume.

"So then, you repented, Martin?"

"Not then—only now. Otherwise there would be no point in telling you this."

"So—it is finished?"

"No, it is not. I gave up any sort of fighting at all when I stopped my quarreling with God. I let the world push me—well, mostly. Certainly, I let Rainald push me. I became a coward. He even made me marry once more! I wanted no part of Ermentrude. She was nothing to me. God knows, she was no beauty. My loins never warmed at the sight—at the thought of her. But he would have killed her out of some insane wish to humiliate me and to make me guilty of her blood.

"So I married her. But I never cared for her that much, not really. I felt sorry for her. She was a good woman. We did the sort of things that a man and wife do in bed—but not very frequently. It was never like it was for me with Claire or with Therese. I think that Ermentrude knew that. But so long as she seemed content, I never bothered to offer more. I felt guilty about that sometimes, but I was afraid to let my feelings get to the point where they would tempt God to strike at me once more.

"But He did anyway, didn't He? You know, after He killed her, I began to care for Ermentrude for the first time. Up until then, it never even occurred to me to ask her if she was pregnant."

"She was not, Martin, although she would have liked to be. Ermentrude spoke to me often about that wish. It was a foolish wish and she knew it. There was no chance, on the pilgrim road and in her physical condition, that the child would have survived. She just loved you. She wanted to be your wife in every way.

"Ermentrude was more than content with what you gave her, Martin. She herself had a strong suspicion that she was dying. More than that, I don't think that there was anyone in the entire pilgrim band who thought that she would last until we reached Santiago. So you see, her death was predestined before you even joined us. If anything, your care lengthened her life. Whatever may have been your own motives before God, don't reproach yourself on her behalf."

Martin made no immediate response to the little priest. He shifted about and poked tentatively at the coals. The wind had become colder and the damp more pervasive. It would be a bad night for sleep.

"There is also the other matter. I killed Rainald. True enough, he wanted me to. I think it amused him that it was me who had to do it. The man was afraid of nothing but of the specter of being humiliated. Those bandits would have killed him very slowly. There would have been much pain. But, I was sure of it then and I am now still, he was more frightened of the ignominy of being killed by a handful of peasant bandits.

"So I killed him. With God as my judge, I bore him no hatred. He was a cruel man, an evil man. You could say that he deserved to die but that is not why I killed him. I felt pity for him. I did it, at his bidding, to spare him the one kind of death that he could not face.

"That's strange, isn't it? I married for him. I killed other men for him. Finally, I killed Rainald himself, at his own wish. Do you think it possible, Simon, that God chose the knight to test how far my own degradation might be pushed? Just because I had stopped fighting Him—refused to resist Him any further—He found a substitute to pursue me. There was never any escape. There isn't now."

"But you have come back here tonight. You are going to complete your pilgrim vow tomorrow. You have confessed yourself just now. Is it over?"

Martin let his breath escape in a long, low exhalation. There was a break in the cloud masses above and the stars of fall were clear in the skies for the moment.

"I don't think that it will ever be over. Nor do I know where it will lead. That's why I'm here with you tonight, Simon. There doesn't seem to be any way to just lay it all down. I have thought of suicide more than once. Back in León after Ermentrude died. Just yesterday by the sea. Rainald, you know, suggested that it was the best thing that I could do. Maybe that's what holds me back from it. So I came here and have confessed to you instead."

Simon was fairly certain that, this time, his big friend had said as much as he was going to say. The little priest stirred himself, and looked carefully away. He did not want to be interrupted.

"Listen to me now, Martin. I will give you absolution in a few moments. It seems to me that what you have said indicates repentence—in some fashion or other. But what I am going to tell you now might prepare you—might help you—to let go of all that past which torments you so.

"You know that I hated Rainald. When you rode back into camp that morning with the news of his death, I was glad for it. God forgive me! It is no business of a priest to hate the other creatures of God. Yet I did.

"If I were to say that it was because the knight was a sinner, that would be both a truth and a lie. It was more than that. Part of my hatred was due to the fact that he humiliated me regularly—as you yourself know. Another part of it grew out of my hatred of myself for being such a coward in his face. I was terrified of him and he exulted in that. You know all about that too. You protected me from him as best you could.

"But there is more yet. This all began before you even joined us. You will remember that I told you of my conviction that Rainald had killed Gerald, the young priest who had helped me organize the pilgrimage. True enough, I hated Rainald because he was the murderer of my dearest friend. Yet even that is not the entire truth.

"Let me begin by saying that I am one of those priests who has never had a problem with women. I was ordained young. I was clear about my wishes in life. I do know what desire for them feels like when the flesh is in its season. Oh yes, no one is spared that experience whether he likes it or not. But I have never been tempted to take a wife and only seldom to take a mistress. At home, many of my fellow priests made sport of me for my solitary ways.

"But Gerald troubled me from the first. He was so young and so handsome. He was so good. Working with him, I came to count his friendship as something very dear. We were very close.

"When we started on the pilgrimage, that began to bother me more than ever. I worried that I loved him too much. I feared that, at some point, I might let my affection for him develop into a physical relationship that would end by destroying us both. Not that Gerald ever encouraged me. He was, I think, a true innocent. Nevertheless, I came daily to fear that if he did encourage me, I might be weak enough to respond to him. I was terrified and yet excited, to tell the truth, by that possibility. My fears grew worse as the days passed.

"And then, he disappeared. I was furious, horrified, and despairing. I knew who had murdered him and why. But I was secretly relieved as well! So long as he was dead, our affection for one another was safe. I no longer had to fear the prospect of a choice between our friendship and my uncertain physical impulses.

"The ultimate salt in my wounds was my conviction that Rainald understood all of this torment of mine. He was so terribly, terribly clever! What he spoke, the way that he expressed it, gave me to think that he understood my divided feelings about Gerald and that he divined, as well, that I was almost half-relieved that his murder had solved my own dilemma.

"The man despised me—and his sneer informed me that he well comprehended just how much I deserved to be despised. Often I was convinced that he must be possessed by at least one devil to be so clever in his evil.

"So you see, Martin, how happy I was when you killed him. I would have wished that it was another who had accomplished it—for your sake. But even if it brought you a greater burden of guilt, I rejoiced at his death. Now the other day, when you had gone off and before I completed my pilgrim's vow, I confessed all of this filth. I am done with it. I have told you of it so that you might understand that you have not been alone in your search. If you will reflect for a moment or two, I will give you absolution.

"Ego te absolvo . . . ."

The two men sat in silence for a bit. The cathedral bells in their rickety tower began slowly to toll. The night was far enough advanced so that the monks of the enclosure were being awakened to perform matins and lauds, the first of the canonical hours of the beginning new day. Neither of the friends was ready to sleep, despite the lateness of the hour for all but the devoted ascetics. The clouds had commenced to deliver their long-promised rain but, surprisingly, it was drifting down in the most tentative of mists rather than the expected torrents. Both men had drawn their blankets up over their heads for protection. They could not see one another directly now without consciously turning.

"What will you do now, Martin?"

"In the morning I shall complete my own vow, hear Mass, and reverence the relics of the Blessed James."

"And then? Will you find another group with which to return to France?"

"No, Simon, I will never return to France. That part of my life is over. Many parts of my life have finished, I think. There is no way to restart them and I would fear that God might once more take up His pursuit of me if I did. I am not sure yet that I have forgiven Him but, be that as it may, I will stay here and try to find out what it is that He wants of me.

"There is here, next to the cathedral, a monastery dedicated to Saint Martin whose monks also attend to the daily service of the shrine of the saint and of the pilgrims who visit it. You have seen it, I suppose. Well, I have taken the name of the place as a sign. When I have finished with my proper vow, I intend to ask them for admission in any capacity that seems fitting to them. I hope to end my days here."

His little friend plucked up his courage. To make it the more difficult for the other to refuse, he turned full-face to him in the gloom and rain.

"If you will hear of it, my friend, I will join you in that life. There is nothing back at home for me. I have the feeling that the pilgrimage has led me, as it has yourself, to that place where I am supposed to be. The monks of Saint Martin's will have us, I think. But I want you to decide whether or not we will continue our journey together, you and I. Ever since you joined us, outside of Jaca in the spring, you have led, and it is fitting that you do so now."

For the first time since the evening began, Martin smiled. Then he positively grinned in the darkness. Reaching across, he took the hands of the little priest in his own.

"Done, Simon, done!"